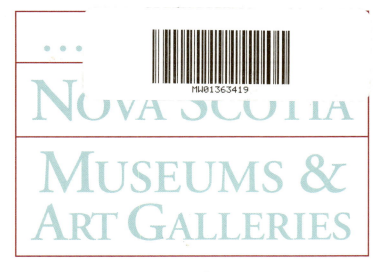

Nova Scotia
Museums & Art Galleries

Allan Lynch

Co-published by
The Province of Nova Scotia
and Nimbus Publishing Limited

Copyright © Allan Lynch, 1998

All rights reserved. No part of this book may be reproduced, stored in a retrieval system or transmitted in any form or by any means without the prior written permission from the co-publishers, or, in the case of photocopying or other reprographic copying, permission from CANCOPY (Canadian Copyright Licensing Agency), 6 Adelaide Street East, Suite 900, Toronto, Ontario, M5C 1H6.

Co-published by the Province of Nova Scotia
and Nimbus Publishing Limited.
Sponsored by:

Economic Development and Tourism
A product of the Nova Scotia Government Co-publishing Program

Design: Arthur Carter, Halifax
Cover Photo: Courtesy of the Nova Scotia Museum
Photo Credits: On the following pages, images are courtesy of the Nova Scotia Museum: 3, 5, 7, 8, 11, 12, 19, 20 (bottom), 25, 28, 31, 52 (top), 56, 65, 74, 75, 88, 90 (bottom), 93, 94. On the following pages, images are courtesy of the museum or gallery: 4, 18, 27, 32, 41, 45, 54 (by Mike Hunter), 65, 66, 67, 68, 69, 70 (bottom), 72, 78, 79, 80, 81, 82, 85, 91, 92, 95. All other images are courtesy of Nova Scotia Economic Development and Tourism.

Printed and bound by Printcrafters Inc.

Canadian Cataloguing in Publication Data
Lynch, Allan
Discover Nova Scotia museums and art galleries
Co-published by N. S. Dept. of Economic Development and Tourism.
Includes bibliographical references and index.
ISBN 1-55109-250-6

1. Museums—Nova Scotia—Guidebooks. 2. Art museums—Nova Scotia—Guidebooks. 3. Nova Scotia—Guidebooks.
I. Nova Scotia. Dept. of Economic Development and Tourism.
II. Title.

FC2303.5.L96   1998   917.1604'4   C97-950255-1
F1037.L96   1998

Dedication
To Sheldon Currie, with apologies for excluding Margaret's Museum.

Nimbus Publishing acknowledges the financial assistance of the Canada Council and the Department of Canadian Heritage.

Contents

Introduction iv

Evangeline Trail 1

Glooscap Trail 21

Sunrise Trail 29

Cape Breton Trails 37

    Cabot Trail 38

    Bras d'Or Lakes Scenic Drive 43

    Fleur-de-lis Trail, Marconi Trail & Metro Cape Breton 46

Marine Drive 55

Halifax Metro Area 63

Lighthouse Route 83

Index 98

Introduction

Pablo Picasso once said, "Give me a museum and I'll fill it." Nova Scotians seem to have wholeheartedly embraced Picasso's philosophy—museums, historic sites, archives, and art galleries are scattered around the province. And Nova Scotians are richer for it.

It should come as no surprise that one of the first parts of North America to be settled by Europeans bears such reverence for the past. For most Nova Scotians the historic past is so pervasive that it's almost invisible—it's simply a part of everyday life. We live in centuries-old homes, work amid equally old buildings, and celebrate traditional music.

Nova Scotia has somehow, perhaps inadvertently, managed to keep history alive. Our museums, rather than being simply repositories for valuable and rare items, are lively and often interactive homes to a type of grass-roots scholarship. We may not recognize it, at first blush, as scholarship—it sounds weighty, something reserved for a lecture hall—but we have managed to represent history without making knowledge intimidating or dull.

Leading the way for this grass roots scholarship is the Nova Scotia Museum. Many provinces and states have "a museum" where the region's significant items are preserved.

The Nova Scotia Museum is a decentralized system of sites. It is not just one building in the capital, Halifax, but a series of twenty-five sites across the province. Their number and collection size show that Nova Scotians don't celebrate just one lifestyle or one heritage. Our system celebrates, studies, and portrays everyone. It is inclusive. The Nova Scotia Museum covers Mi'kmaq, United Empire Loyalists, Celts, Blacks, Acadians, French, British, and so-called "friendly foreign protestants."

And the Nova Scotia Museum is intellectually all-encompassing: it doesn't just represent the romantic lives of the elite who lived in luxury with servants, position, and wealth. These people are represented in grand homes like the Uniacke Estate, Clifton, and Shand House. But the Nova Scotia Museum also includes the workers, the tradespeople, and the poor. These people may not have been included in the old written histories, but they have contributed to this province's history through their work and sacrifice. It is these people's stories which remind us of the dignity of work and the texture of our history.

There are many intriguing museum sites outside the Nova Scotia Museum. Nova Scotia is endowed with many individual community museums, such as the Yarmouth County Museum and the Springhill Miners' Museum, and federally operated Parks Canada sites, such as Fort Anne National Historic Site and Fortress Louisbourg, which speak about the province's history from various perspectives.

Art galleries are another avenue to Nova Scotia's history and culture. Galleries, many of them community-based, abound across the province. They feature work by local artists and a range in styles from folk art to installations, from photography to quilts. These galleries reveal innovation alongside tradition.

Nova Scotia's diverse cultural roots enrich museum collections and gallery exhibits. The Mi'kmaq lived in harmony with the land until their way of life was irrevocably altered with the coming of European settlers. Power struggles between the French and British not only shaped the history of the province but the lives of those who were caught in the middle. The Mi'kmaq and Acadians were dramatically affected and much was lost by both cultures.

Nova Scotia has been enriched by the influx over the centuries of those seeking to escape religious and political persecution, such as the Scots, Irish, Germans, Blacks, Loyalists, and Planters. The province's museums and art galleries bear witness to the waves of change so that we might look on the past and reflect in order to look ahead with understanding and insight.

The joke in Nova Scotia is that we have so many museums because people don't throw anything out, they just put up a building to house it. And good for us. Exploring Nova Scotia's museums and art collections is an enriching experience, thanks to Nova Scotians who adopted Picasso's boast.

This book does not profile all facilities. When the research for it began there were 249 facilities and three more opened during the summer of 1997. The museums and galleries profiled are representative of the history and culture available to the public in Nova Scotia. This guidebook is meant to whet an appetite. The goal is to inspire visitors and residents to explore the province's history and arts. If one community's museum is profiled and another is not this is no reflection on the quality of the collection or presentation. Arbitrary constraints, such as time and space, limited which facilities are profiled.

Like a map, this book is a starting point, a way to look at Nova Scotia. There are more treasures and joys to discover along the highways, lanes, and backroads.

Note: Some sites include maps that are from various sources and therefore not of a consistent scale. Maps to scale include: the Scenic Travelways Map (scale: 1:64,000), available from Visitor Information Centres around the province; *Map of the Province of Nova Scotia* (scale: 1:250,000) available in bookstores; and topographical maps (scales: 1:50,000 and 1:250,000), available from the Government Bookstore.

Symbols

- Washroom
- Accessible
- **PA** Partly Accessible
- Parking
- Food
- Picnic Area
- Admission
- Information
- National park/site
- Provincial site
- Non-profit group
- Gift shop/kiosk
- Archives
- Bilingual services

Evangeline Trail

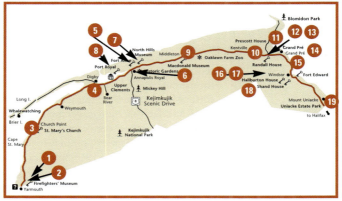

1. Yarmouth County Museum Complex
2. Firefighters' Museum of Nova Scotia
3. Gallerie Père-Leger-Comeau & Musée Ste-Marie
4. Admiral Digby Museum
5. Fort Anne National Historic Site
6. O'Dell House Museum
7. North Hills Museum
8. Port Royal National Historic Site
9. Annapolis Valley Macdonald Museum
10. Old Kings Courthouse Museum
11. Prescott House Museum
12. Randall House Museum
13. Acadia University Art Gallery
14. Grand Pré National Historic Site
15. Fort Edward National Historic Site
16. Shand House Museum
17. Windsor Hockey Heritage Museum
18. Haliburton House Museum
19. Uniacke Estate Museum Park

Yarmouth County Museum Complex

The Yarmouth County Museum collection includes an artifact attributed to Vikings and fine artifacts from Yarmouth's early days as a major shipping port.

In early European settlement, location was everything. Yarmouth's location—as a bridge between the British colonies and the American States—made it a major shipping port. As a result of the port activity a strong manufacturing sector developed and flourished along with the shipping and fishing industries.

Prosperity meant residents, many of whom were New England Planters and United Empire Loyalists, built grand homes and filled them with even grander objects. Today, the Yarmouth County Museum, the recipient of many of these items, boasts one of the most interesting collections in the province.

The Yarmouth County Museum is housed in an old church. From the outside it evokes the craftsmen school of architecture. Inside it clearly shows the shipwrights' craftsmanship: men who built ships used the same construction techniques to erect this church.

(902) 742-5539
Open June 1–Oct. 15
Mon.–Sat. 9–5
Sun. 2–5;
Oct. 16–May 31
Tues.–Sat. 2–5

The museum collection ranges from the Runic stone—believed to have been carved by Vikings in 1,000 A.D.—to the giant 170-prism lighthouse light, a Victoria Cross, to a 1915 Auto Electric Pleasure Car. There are also large doll, costume, china, and glass collections. Since this was a busy port, there is a large collection of travel items: chests, cases, and ship's items including old menus, which are fun to read. There is also a large collection of ship paintings, musical instruments (accordions to zithers), and Mi'kmaq artifacts.

Fuller House & Killam Office open in summer only

Next door is the Fuller House Museum. Once the "Fuller Brush Man's" summer home, it is now open to the public. The third part of the museum complex is the Killam Bros. Shipping Office, dating back to the mid-1800s.

Directions: YMC is at 22 Collins Street, Fuller House at 20 Collins Street, and the Killam Shipping Office is across from the ferry terminal at 90 Water Street.

Discover Nova Scotia Museums and Art Galleries

Firefighters' Museum of Nova Scotia

Other than Fire Prevention Week or personal tragedy, most people probably don't stop to think about fire fighting.

The Firefighters' Museum of Nova Scotia in Yarmouth shows us exactly how complicated firefighting can be. From the founding of the first settlements, fear of fire was an issue. And no wonder: wooden buildings, heated by open fireplaces, were closely connected, and water came from wells.

The museum covers three centuries of firefighting history through artifacts, photographs, and anecdotes.

The museum traces firefighting in Nova Scotia from 1700 to the 1950s. Its weird and romantic collection ranges from ancient fire trumpets (used to shout orders or as a bludgeon in "tempestuous situations") to red-shirted men with their Dalmatians.

Expectations of big red machines are fufilled. The surprise is a collection of not-so-big early steam engines, which look like furnaces on wheels dominated by a huge smoke stack. Machines like the 1863 Amoskeag Steamer and the 1880 chrome and brass Silsby Steamer replaced bucket brigades by pumping water faster and dousing flames more quickly. The oldest "engine" in the collection is the 1819 Hopwood & Tilley hand engine made in London. It looks like a horse trough on wheels, more folk art than fire engine.

One of the most amazing displays tells of how communities as early as 1700 built fire mains from hollowed out logs laid underground. When firemen needed water they drilled a hole into the main and plugged it after the fire was out. This is why fire hydrants are often referred to as plugs.

The collection also carries brigade banners, fire toys, old hydrants, and fire warden staffs. The Firefighters' Museum is a time capsule for three hundred years of social history and technological advancement.

Directions: The Firefighters' Museum is at 451 Main Street, Yarmouth.

(902) 742-5525
Open year-round
June 1–Oct. 15
Mon.–Sat. 9-5;
July and Aug.
Mon.–Sat. 9–9
Sun. 10–5;
Oct. 16–May 31
Mon.–Sat. 9–4
Sun. 1–4

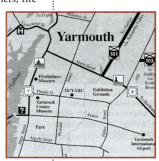

Gallerie Père-Leger-Comeau & Musée Ste-Marie

Gallerie Père-Leger-Comeau is at the Université Ste. Anne, in Church Point. It is a new exhibition space for local artists. There is no permanent collection or set calendar for student exhibition. There are also few rules. Local artists are free to book the space to present their own exhibitions. Hours vary depending on the artist's availability.

The Père-Leger-Comeau Gallery is located on Nova Scotia's only French university campus.

Church Point is also the location of St. Mary's Church, the largest wooden church in North America. Augustine Regneault, who designed the castle-like edifice, was influenced by the famous chateaux of the Loire Valley, near his home in Rennes, France. Completed in 1905, the church houses Musée Ste-Marie (St. Mary's Museum) featuring church furnishings, documents, and photographs. Artifacts include a wooden clapper (used instead of a bell) and an 1806 Altar Stone.

Each first Sunday of September, the congregation pays tribute to those who planned and built the church and to those who continue to maintain it.

Directions: The gallery is located in the university administration building behind the reception area. The church is adjacent to the university.

Gallery
Call (902) 769-2114 for details about gallery hours and current exhibitions.

Church & museum
(902) 769-2808
Open June 1–Oct. 13 daily 9–5;
other times by appointment.
The church is partly accessible.

Admiral Digby Museum

The Admiral Digby Museum brochure promises visitors "more than just old stuff!" But, the Admiral Digby is full of old stuff, just as any self-respecting museum would be. Much of the "old stuff" relates to local history and industry, especially shipbuilding and the fishery. The collection includes sailors' accoutrements—sextants, spy glasses, sail mender's case—wooden ship models, and a display dedicated to an economic mainstay: the scallop industry. There's even a 1928 patent for a scallop rake.

Those with ink in their veins will enjoy the print room, with the wood block type and foot powered press. Upstairs is a large photo collection tracing Digby's role in tourism. Today the Pines Resort attracts tourists to the community; in the past visitors came to establishments like the Manhattan Hotel. There is also a telling costume collection (when women's waists measured 17 in.) covering the period 1865 to the 1940s.

The Admiral Digby Museum is named for Robert Digby who led a flotilla of United Empire Loyalists here in 1783. The museum also maintains a Loyalist archive and genealogy as well as a small gallery featuring local artists. The original township map in the hall was a gift of the Edison family to the community. Thomas Edison's family arrived in Digby in 1763.

The highlight of the Digby collection is the Gilpin watercolours. These twelve paintings were done by Dr. Gilpin who went to Sable Island to deliver a baby. The lighthouse keeper's wife had lost a previous child, and the doctor wanted to see her through a successful birth. Gilpin went to Sable Island on May 3, 1854 and stayed until July 22, 1854, presumably to paint.

This is a small museum full of surprises, some old, some not so old.

Directions: The museum is at 95 Montague Row, across from the tourist information office.

Displays on shipbuilding and the fishery reflect local history.

(902) 245-6322
Open mid-June–
Aug. 31
9–5 daily;
limited hours in
September (1–4);
other times by
appointment

5 Fort Anne National Historic Site

Armies often maintained the victor's spoils, adding the newly won fort or town to its defences. This is what happened at Fort Anne National Historic Site in Annapolis Royal.

The area around what is now Annapolis Royal was first settled and developed by the French. During years of imperial struggle between the British and French, the community was the site of fifteen battles and changed hands five times.

A strategic site, Fort Anne changed hands five times between the British and French.

Annapolis Royal is one of the key communities, along with Halifax, Louisbourg, and Grand Pré, in the history of Nova Scotia. In 1629 the Scots built Charles Fort here, followed by the French, who were routed by New Englanders. Named for Queen Anne, it remained the colony's capital until Halifax was founded in 1749.

The present defensive structure was built in 1779 on orders from Queen Victoria's father, the Duke of Kent, who was in charge of the garrison in Halifax, and used until 1854. While older than the Halifax Citadel, Fort Anne is built on the same star-shaped principle using earthen walls to camouflage the fortress. This type of structure was virtually impenetrable to cannon fire.

(902) 532-2397
Open May 15–Oct.15 daily 9–6;
off-season group tours available by arrangement

Inside the museum building displays focus on interpretation panels which use a series of quotes and vignettes along with a few artifacts to tell the history of Annapolis Royal.

Two prize items are the Fort Anne Heritage Tapestry designed by Kiyoko Grenier-Saso, which took 20,000 hours to complete, and the 1621 Royal Charter of Nova Scotia. The only other copy of this document is in Edinburgh Castle.

Visitors can explore the grounds free of charge. The Garrison graveyard on the property has the first tombstones in Canada.

Directions: The site is in downtown Annapolis Royal on George Street.

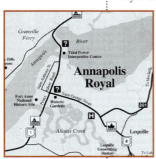

O'Dell House Museum

Annapolis Royal's whole downtown is practically a museum. Since it was once the colonial capital, there are dozens of historically important and interesting buildings throughout the town.

One such building is the O'Dell House Museum. Once a tavern and inn, the O'Dell is again arranged to resemble a traveller's rest stop. Entered through the tavern, the downstairs looks as it did when it accepted guests. Upstairs a bedroom is arranged like the original hotel room and displays the Victorian accoutrements required for travel.

What stands out at this museum is a small upstairs room dedicated to Victorian mourning practices. It could be a set for Masterpiece Theatre's Mystery series. The floor is painted black, and the dark wallpaper is covered in mourning wreaths made from the hair of the deceased.

Other remembrances include mourning dresses and grim, large wicker baskets. These casket-sized wicker baskets were a Victorian body bag used to transport the deceased to the undertaker.

There is also a small display devoted to the so-called "Fairy Sisters," Cassie and Victoria Foster. These twin girls each weighed 1 lb. at birth and were two of eleven children born to the Foster family. A rare genetic disorder caused every second Foster child to be born a midget. By age 12 Cassie Foster weighed only 12 lbs. Her 17-year-old brother Dudley weighed only 10 lbs. Their shoes and chair illustrate how frail, small, and delicate these children were. It's a fascinating and sobering display.

The O'Dell Museum may appear ordinary from the outside, but like a gift, it's full of surprises inside.

Directions: Locate the bright yellow building past the wharf on St. George Street, Annapolis Royal.

Formerly a stagecoach inn and tavern, O'Dell House accommodated Victorian travellers.

(902) 532-7754
Open June 1–Sept. 30
Mon.–Sat. 9:30–5
Sun. 1–5

North Hills Museum

If good things come in small packages, really good things must come in plain buildings. Near Granville Ferry, the North Hills Museum, on the road to the Habitation at Port Royal, has one of the most stunning collections of fine Georgian furniture, glass, ceramics, and silver to be found anywhere on the Eastern Seaboard.

This unassuming little house was built in 1764 and enhanced over the years. Two hundred years later, Toronto antique dealer Robert Patterson saw the potential of this dilapidated house and set about creating the country retreat he longed for.

Restoring the property was a labour of love, which helped soften the costs—authenticity isn't cheap. Patterson created a gorgeous library, with floor-to-ceiling bookshelves, exposed beams, fireplace, and filled with comfortable chintz-covered chairs. The dining room is right out of the English countryside, as is the formal parlour.

This is one man's private collection, assembled with great care and foresight. It ranges from Lalique vases, free blown glass, New Hall Porcelain, tea caddies, to landscapes and portraits by members of the Royal Academy. The furniture is made of mahogany, walnut, oak, and the absolutely exotic, very rare oyster wood. (Oyster wood is walnut cut across the grain to look like flattened shells.)

The furniture represents the work of Sheraton, Chippendale, and Hepplewhite, plus the Georgian fashion of Japanned furniture.

North Hills is here because one man was able to fulfill his dream of an elegant retirement surrounded by history and beautiful things.

Although unassuming on the exterior, North Hills Museum contains rare and luxury items.

(902) 532-2168
Open June 1–Oct.15
Mon.–Sat. 9:30–5:30
Sun. 1–5:30

Directions: Follow Route 1 to Granville Ferry, Proceed 1.5 km (1 mi.) beyond Granville Ferry to the North Hills Museum, along the road to the Habitation at Port Royal.

Discover Nova Scotia Museums and Art Galleries

Port Royal National Historic Site

Officially the Port Royal National Historic Site (a.k.a. the Habitation) is a "compound" consisting of a series of buildings abutting each other, around a courtyard, with heavily barracked entrance, palisade, and cannon platform.

The compound was built in 1605, after half the members of a French expedition died during the winter spent on St. Croix Island in the St. Croix River. The survivors crossed the Bay of Fundy looking for a milder climate and easy relationship with the Mi'kmaq.

The Habitation was founded as a fur trading post under Pierre Du Gua de Monts though he is often overshadowed in history by his cartographer, Samuel de Champlain. The original compound was destroyed by a group of Virginians in 1613.

Wandering through the buildings, visitors see the different lifestyles and social classes of the inhabitants. The governor's residence has a huge fireplace, heavy furniture, and a separate upstairs bedroom. Even though this upstairs room is dark and musty, it was the greatest luxury in the new world at the time. The other gentlemen in the company lived in rooms off the courtyard.

The "commoners" lived in a dark upstairs barrack, sleeping in bunks or hammocks. Should one have the misfortune of falling ill, he was put into an isolation chamber—a large pine box away from the others.

Visitors should take greatest note of the common room. Canadian winters were such a shock for the French that to boost morale, Champlain invented the Order of Good Cheer. Each member of the colony was responsible for putting on a banquet and evening entertainment. This inspired a competition to see who could give the best party which laid roots of that lasting Maritime tradition: the desire to have a good time.

Directions: Port Royal is across the bay from Annapolis Royal, follow the signs. The site is well marked.

Canada's first theatrical performance, *Theatre Neptune* took place at the Habitation.

(902) 532-2321
Open daily
May 15–Oct. 15
9–6

Annapolis Valley Macdonald Museum

A newer building than the school Macdonald founded continues to educate. Check out the natural history collection in the greenhouse.

(902) 825-6116
Open year-round
May 15–Oct.15
Mon.–Sat. 9–5
Sun. 1-5;
Oct. 16–May 14
Mon.–Fri. 10:30–5
(subject to change)

The former head of the Macdonald Tobacco Company in Montreal, Christopher Macdonald, believed in practical education, that students learned by doing as much as by study. As a result Macdonald provided funds to establish modern schools all across Canada and Middleton benefited from his philanthropy.

When the school Macdonald founded was replaced by a newer building, residents opted to keep the education aspect alive by converting the building into the Annapolis Valley Macdonald Museum.

Typically, the museum collection focuses on local history and artifacts. However, what makes this museum sing is its extensive clock collection; the Macdonald Museum has an impressive collection of timepieces. The number and types of clocks are staggering. There are English longcase clocks (often mistaken for grandfather clocks), Black Forest Clocks, shelf clocks, pillar & scroll, looking-glass, "ogee," steeple, mantle, drop, Grecian, calendar, ships', dome, carriage, and novelty clocks.

Coincidentally, the collection ties the large clock-making industry which flourished in New England to Haliburton House in Windsor. Judge Thomas Chandler Haliburton was the foremost humorist of his age, having made a reputation writing about the roguish clock peddler Sam Slick. The Macdonald Museum even has the type of clocks Slick sold.

Beyond the chorus of clocks, the Macdonald Museum has an interesting natural history collection, which gives a snapshot look at the topological diversity of the Annapolis Valley.

As a former schoolhouse, the museum has a lot of floor space. Upstairs are several galleries for historic displays such as a 1940s classroom, plus an art gallery featuring local and Nova Scotian artists in changing exhibitions.

The Macdonald Museum has a refreshingly different collection from many local museums.

Directions: Take Exit 18 and follow the museum signs to 21 School Street in Middleton.

Old Kings Courthouse Museum

Three events have shaped modern-day Kings County: reclamation of land from the sea by the Acadians, deportation of the Acadians in 1755, and arrival of New England Planters in 1759. These events are the primary focus of the Old Kings Courthouse Museum, Kentville.

Planter and Acadian history is highlighted with an interactive model, archives, and film.

Originally built to house the Kings County law courts, this Georgian style building contains three floors of display space. In the basement is the Kings Historical Society Family History Archives, which includes a substantial genealogical collection on Planter families.

The main floor focuses on the Planter legacy. This includes a thirty-minute film about Planter life. The arrival of eight thousand New England Planters, which began in 1779, was important for economic and military purposes because this was the first major immigration of English speaking people into what is now Canada.

The second floor displays show how the Acadians constructed 240 km (149 mi.) of dykes to reclaim 17,000 ha (42,000 acres) of land from the Minas Basin. The earthen mounds seen lining the county's rivers and shoreline may seem like a simple engineering project by today's standards, but at the time they were an ancient megaproject for a peasant people working with only their hands and a few oxen.

The display includes a small interactive model which simulates a rainstorm to show how the Acadian system of aboiteaux—a type of sluice gate made from hollowed-out logs—worked to drain water from the protected land and keep sea water out. It's a fascinating display for all ages, but stand back or get wet.

The museum also hosts travelling exhibitions.

The Kings Courthouse Museum is a first stop in tracing the Planter immigration and settlement. Consider it a companion destination to Grand Pré.

(902) 678-6237
Open year-round
Sept.–April
Tues.–Fri. 9:30–4:30;
May–June
Mon.–Fri. 9:30–4:30;
July and Aug.
Mon.–Fri. 9:30–4:30
Sat. 11:30–4:30

Directions: Follow Route 1, the Evangeline Trail, to Kentville. The museum is at 37 Cornwallis Street.

Evangeline Trail 11

Prescott House Museum

(902) 542-3984
Open: Apple Blossom Weekend (end of May) to Oct. 15, Mon.–Sat. 9:30–5:30
Sun. 1–5:30

Looking at Prescott House in Starr's Point today, it's impossible to imagine anyone could use it as a barn. This elegant Georgian house looks too grand to have ever been used to store hay and farm implements, so perhaps it is to the builder's credit that this structure could survive such use. Today Prescott House looms through the trees that were intentionally planted to set off the imposing structure.

Named Acacia Grove, the house was built in the early 1800s by Charles Prescott, a successful Halifax  merchant. Having secured his fortune, and suffering from poor health, he moved to the gentler valley climate to become a politician and gentleman farmer. Prescott was such an accomplished tree expert that he is credited with establishing the province's large commercial apple industry. A Maritime Johnny Appleseed, Prescott planted trees and orchards, experimented with crops, and developed species for this climate, most notably the Gravenstein.

After Prescott's death in 1859, the house had a number of owners and uses. It was eventually restored by Prescott's great-granddaughter, Mary, who returned Acacia Grove to its former glory when guests included the colonial elite, like the Lieutenant-Governor, the Earl of Dalhousie.

Now a museum, Prescott House bears the symmetry Georgians loved. There is a central hall and large, bright rooms, painted in inventive colour schemes (like forest green and oyster). There is a fine furniture collection, a substantial number of samplers, and an extensive array of fabrics. Be sure to look at the front door lock—it's a wonder anyone could lift the key!

A tour of this house is more like a chance to sneak through a neighbour's home with people who know their secrets. It's very personal and great fun.

Directions: Prescott House Museum is located at 1633 Starr's Point Road. Follow the signs from Port Williams.

Prescott House is an intimate look at one famous Nova Scotian's life. The grounds are delightful, the interior exquisite.

Randall House Museum

The Town of Wolfville has always been a prosperous community. Its financial comfort comes from the stability of the rich agricultural land surrounding the town, its role as an educational centre, and as a port, although Wolfville has the smallest harbour in Canada and ships have long since stopped coming here.

Across from three hundred-year-old dykes built by the Acadians who first lived here is the Randall House Museum. This community-owned facility aims to represent life in Wolfville from 1760 to 1960.

Randall House has somehow escaped tampering with its historical purity to remain a prime, rare example of vintage Nova Scotia architecture. Built for and lived in by three generations of a Planter family, Randall House shows how average people lived: neither grand nor poverty-stricken, the householders lived comfortably.

Randall House is a classic example of how average Planter families lived in the area over three generations.

The museum has a large textile collection. There's also an extensive button collection. When money was scarce, women used elaborate buttons in the place of jewellery to decorate their clothing. Randall House's collection ranges from cameos and jewels to insects and lobsters to cupids and cherubs, and mermaids.

The museum's contents follow an 1836 household inventory attached to a previous owner's will.

One of the rarer items in the collection is a dump cart saddle. The saddle helped horses handle heavy loads more easily. In the mid-1800s every house had one. Because they were so common, many of these saddles were simply tossed out, making them into something they never were: rare.

(902) 542-9775
Open June 15–
Sept. 15
Mon.–Fri. 10–5
Sun. 2–5

Directions: The museum is located at 171 Main Street, Wolfville, next to the park and tourist bureau. There is parking available on the street.

13 Acadia University Art Gallery

The Acadia University Art Gallery, in Wolfville, covers a broad spectrum of regional, national, and international art in a variety of mediums. Exhibits feature historical as well as contemporary work. Exhibits change regularly.

See local and international artists' works at the university art gallery, on the Acadia campus, in the heart of Wolfville.

Directions: The gallery is located in the Beveridge Arts Centre on the corner of Highland and Main Streets.

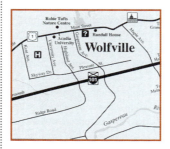

(902) 585-1373
Open June 1–Aug 31 daily 12–5;
rest of the year open weekdays 11–5 and weekends 1–4

Grand Pré National Historic Site

For the Acadians, Grand Pré is a sacred place where their ancestors once built a thriving, close-knit farm community. On September 10, 1755, Grand Pré was ripped apart when Lieutenant-Colonel John Winslow read the Deportation Order. Summoned to the parish church, the village men expected to be asked, once again, to pledge allegiance to the British Crown. However, this time the scenario did not play out as it had in the past.

Grand Pré National Historic Site is primarily a contemplative place with sprawling lawns, flower gardens, and huge weeping willows.

The English, having fought so many wars with the French, never fully trusted the passive Acadians, who were of French ancestry. The British saw the potential for their worst nightmare to come true when they captured Fort Beauséjour and found Acadians helping behind the palisades. So when the Acadian men refused once again to swear allegiance to the British king, they were taken prisoner and deported.

Ships arrived across the dykelands to disperse the ten thousand Acadians among the British colonies from New England to Louisiana. The event is the basis for Longfellow's epic poem about lost love, "Evangeline."

The focal point of the Grand Pré site is the reconstructed stone church. Inside is a series of paintings which depict Acadian life and the Deportation. Outside, down a lane and facing the old village is the bronze replica of Longfellow's Evangeline. Her face shows the image of two women: the side facing up basks in the sunshine of youth, while the face looking down shows a woman worn by hardship and sorrow.

(902) 542-3631
Open May 15–Oct. 15
daily 9–6

Grand Pré has shifted emphasis from static history to memorial site, telling the larger story of the expulsion and celebrating important days in the Acadian calendar. It's not just a place on the map, but part of the soul of a people.

Directions: Grand Pré is located just outside the Town of Wolfville. It is well marked.

15 Fort Edward National Historic Site

Fort Edward National Historic Site resembles the type of toy structure found in the middle of a miniature golf course—putt the ball into the fort and move to the next hole. Perhaps that is why this dark brown blockhouse on the hill is often missed by motorists zipping along Highway 101 past Windsor.

However, it was once a critical element in the colonial defence system. Fort Edward protected the overland route between Halifax and the Bay of Fundy, and fortified the British presence among the large Acadian population that lived around Piziquid.

The fort was constructed in 1750 and abandoned a century later. Fort Edward is the last blockhouse still standing in Nova Scotia and the oldest of its type in Canada. Today Fort Edward, which was named for Edward, Duke of Kent, is a series of plaques explaining the layout of the now deteriorated fort, the blockhouse, and some earthen mounds. It only takes a few minutes to read the plaques, but there are panoramic views of the surrounding area which show why military planners chose this location. This is one of the sites from which Acadians were deported in 1755.

Overlooking Piziquid Basin, Fort Edward was once an important part of British posts between Annapolis Royal and Halifax.

(902) 542-3631
Grounds are open year-round; blockhouse is open

Directions: From Highway 101, take Exit 6. The fort site is on Fort Edward Street, the first left off King Street, near the town hall in Windsor.

Discover Nova Scotia Museums and Art Galleries

Shand House Museum

Approaching Windsor across the causeway from Falmouth, the tall, slender, grey house with it's four-storey tower dominates the view. This Queen Anne style home is the Shand House Museum.

When this house was built in 1890 for newlyweds Clifford and Henrie Shand it was the most modern home in the province. It had indoor plumbing, central heating, and gas lighting. Of all the heritage houses open to the public, Shand House is one of three to include a bathroom. A year later it was one of the first homes converted to electricity.

Among their businesses, Clifford Shand's father was a part owner of the Windsor Furniture Company, which provided furniture specially commissioned for the house.

Inside, the house is a magnificent style statement. It speaks of a type of grace and craftsmanship displaced by so-called modern conveniences. The carvings, mouldings, and wood decorations are as fresh and unmarked as the day the Shands moved in.

The soaring hallway is lined in cherry wood. The dining room is oak. And in an amazingly complicated detail the dining room door is split to match the dining room's oak, and the hall's cherry.

For the hearty and sure-footed, there is a special reward in the fourth-floor tower room. This is where Clifford's son Errol, a great cyclist, used to escape. It provides wonderful views across Lake Piziquid. The steps are steep, so be careful.

Shand House is an unedited look at how the family lived. It is probably one of the most graceful homes on display in Nova Scotia. Don't miss it.

Directions: In Windsor, follow Water Street to the liquor store, then turn up the hill. Shand House is at 389 Avon Street. There is limited parking.

Shand House is a glimpse into "modern" conveniences and upper-middle class lifestyle in Nova Scotia.

(902) 798-8213
Open June 1-Oct. 15
Mon.–Sat. 9:30–5:30
Sun. 1–5:30;
also open Apple Blossom Festival Weekend

Windsor Hockey Heritage Museum

Canada's national game—hockey—started in Windsor. There may be some diehards in Ontario who believe it started elsewhere, but Windsor residents know better.

In his 1836 book, The Clockmaker, Judge Thomas Chandler Haliburton wrote about a game of ball played on the ice. In 1844, he recorded his childhood reminisces of life at King's College School, where as a student in 1800, Haliburton recalled boys "racin', yelpin', hollerin' and whoopin' like mad with pleasure ... with games at base in the fields, or hurley on the long pond on the ice ..." Historians and hockey enthusiasts maintain this passage is the first recorded reference to hockey. (Hurley is an Irish game involving balls and bats.) The Windsor Hockey Heritage Museum supports this contention.

Starr hockey skates, champion style, were developed in Nova Scotia in 1899.

There is a wonderful skate collection, which traces the progression of technology from wooden runners strapped on boots to metal clamps used in the 1890s, and tube skates from 1900.

The museum has fun with the sport, showing how quickly the hurley-on-ice players learned to modify their equipment for the new game. Ribbed white hurley balls, which bounced uncontrollably and became lost in the snow, were replaced by disks cut from a tree. Those disks evolved into the pucks we know today. Oddly, it took one hundred years to develop the hockey net.

Call (902) 798-1800 for hours of operation.

The museum also details the growing popularity of hockey, including that of "ladies' leagues" back in the 1920s and 1930s.

It's a small museum, piled high with old equipment, photos, and trophies. Hockey fans will love this museum and its refreshing slant toward the glory and purity of a great game played for sport; not winning for the sake of winning. It's a moral lesson for a cynical age.

Directions: The museum is now in a storefront in the business section at 118 Gerrish Street, Windsor.

Haliburton House Museum

(902) 798-2915
Open June 1–Oct. 30
Mon.–Sat. 9:30–5:30
Sun. 1–5:30

Many of us are familiar with such expressions as, "Quick as a wink," "It's raining cats and dogs," "Facts are stranger than fiction," and "barking up the wrong tree."

Well, these quirky but common expressions all came from Judge Thomas Chandler Haliburton. More than a bewigged, black-robed magistrate in His Majesty's service, Haliburton was also the leading humorist and best selling author of his day. His books took readers on the ridiculous trail of the fictional wandering Yankee clock peddler, Sam Slick.

Haliburton was the first Canadian author to gain an international reputation. Not only was his work popular with readers in Canada and America, it was even reviewed in the *Illustrated London News.*

His home, Clifton, is approached through iron gates, past a keeper's lodge, up a drive flanked by trees and a pond. It's an elegant villa with a surprisingly large interior. There is a huge foyer-cum-ballroom connected to a formal parlour. The cavernous dining room has a vaulted ceiling which soars toward a central skylight. Almost as large is Haliburton's library.

The interior layout is interesting because it breaks with the traditional style. This is an offbeat mansion, where the main hall runs right to left, not front to back, and bedrooms are arranged in side wings at different levels.

The house is furnished to the 1830–50s period. The furniture is large, formal, and bright, like the house. Many of the walls are decorated with framed cartoons based on Haliburton's writing.

Haliburton House, furnished in mid-Victorian style, reflects the life of renowned author Thomas Haliburton.

Clifton is a serene place, managing to retain just the kind of solitude and quiet a writer cherishes.

Directions: Haliburton House is located at 424 Clifton Avenue, Windsor. Follow the key signs.

Uniacke Estate Museum Park

This property was inspired by the English "park" estate. The house—a rare treasure with its contents fully intact—is a fascinating reflection of the man who built it.

(902) 866-2650
Open June 1–Oct. 15
Mon.–Sat. 9:30–5:30
Sun. 1–5:30

Trails are open year-round, dawn to dusk. Food is available in the tea room/café only in summer.

The Uniacke Estate Museum Park has all the elements of a classic English estate: a long, treed drive that opens onto a rolling field, a lake and a grand mansion. Even at a distance Uniacke House, with its two-storey pillared portico, looks like the home of an important, powerful, and wealthy family.

The estate was built by Richard John Uniacke. Although a well-born Irishman, he was a younger son, with no expectations of inheriting his family's wealth. Uniacke moved to Philadelphia and made the economically advantageous move of marrying his employer's thirteen-year-old daughter.

After moving to Nova Scotia, then back to Ireland to complete his law degree, Uniacke permanently settled in the colony in 1781. He was a successful lawyer, land owner, and politician. But his real wealth came from the fees he earned as Advocate General in the Vice-Admiralty Court.

The position and wealth allowed Uniacke to live like the gentleman he was. He had a Halifax townhouse along with this country estate. At its height the country property comprised 4,800 ha (11,800 acres), a house, barn, carriage house, wash house, grain barn, billiard room, baths, store room, icehouse, hot house, and summer houses. Today the estate consists of the mansion house, two outbuildings, and six hiking trails on 1,010 ha (2500 acres).

Uniacke was a large man with equally large tastes. His tall love seat-sized library chair speaks to Uniacke's "quite broad" 6'2" physique. Inside Uniacke filled his home with people (as many as one hundred at a banquet) and exquisite objects, like the scenic or "philosophical instruments" educated gentlemen used to amuse themselves and guests, the specially commissioned Adams furniture, and fine porcelains.

Uniacke house is more than a collection of objects, it is an intact study of how an important colonial family lived.

Directions: From Highway 103, take Exit 3 to Mount Uniacke. Follow the signs.

Glooscap Trail

20 Heritage Model Centre
21 Springhill Miners' Museum
22 The Anne Murray Centre
23 Fundy Geological Museum
24 Age of Sail Heritage Centre
25 Showcase Nova Scotia
26 Lawrence House Museum

20 Heritage Model Centre

"Bud" Johnston is a hobbyist with time on his hands. His hobby is making scale models of buildings in the River Herbert and Joggins area. As his collection of models grew into a miniature community, residents realized they were a form of historic preservation, since many of the buildings no longer exist outside faded photographs and memories.

The Heritage Model Centre was built to keep the collection together and to preserve it from the elements. (Johnston used to display it on his lawn, until it outgrew his yard.) Each model is built to one-twelfth scale, and while sometimes rough looking, they contain amazing detail.

These meticulous scale models preserve the original structures they represent, some of which no longer exist.

The collection includes models of a sugar camp, the Chignecto Ship Railway, a lumber company, a general store, a bandstand full of pipers, and a fall fair with fully operational rides.

These displays are not simply doll-house-like models. They have animation, sounds, and special effects. The lumber mill, for instance, lights up, saws spin, ropes pull, and men move. The railway round house emits steam as if the engines inside could go chugging across the floor at any moment.

The blacksmith shop is complete, down to the tiny tools and a 1920 calendar. The schoolhouse has papers on the desks and tiny writing on the blackboard. The general store's shelves are stacked with items. For the Royal Theatre, Johnston made 280 individual seats! Each display is backed by a mural to give the building its proper setting and context.

It's a great place to take kids since everything is at their eye level and to a child's scale, and it's great fun for people who love to tinker.

(902) 251-2666
Open mid-May–mid-Oct.
Mon.–Sat. 9–5
Sun. 10–6

Directions: The model centre is at 1868 Main Street, River Herbert, on Route 242.

Springhill Miners' Museum

Cumberland County was blessed with abundant mineral deposits. And one of the main minerals in this part of the province is coal. For many years coal was king, and Springhill was a capital of this kingdom.

The Springhill Miners' Museum tells the history of mining in the area, how coal is mined, and the hazards of underground mining. Springhill suffered four major mining disasters: in 1891, 125 men were killed; in 1916 there was an underground fire; a 1956 explosion took 39 more lives; and the infamous 1958 "bump" which claimed another 75 lives. (A "bump" occurs when pressure forces the floor to hit the ceiling.) Because of these tragedies, a large part of the collection deals with safety measures and artifacts, and the effects of these disasters on individuals and the town.

After viewing the indoor museum, visitors are led into a wash house where a former miner explains the procedure for going into a mine. The third part of the museum experience is to walk 107 m (350 ft.) underground to see a former coal mine and learn about the draconian working conditions.

Many of us know, in theory, that mining is a hard way to make a living. But seeing and hearing how difficult it was from someone who did it brings the grim reality sharply into focus. It's not a large museum, but it can have a huge effect.

Hint: Bring socks for the mine tour, visitors are given rubber boots to wear along with a raincoat and a hard hat. Don't wear light colours.

Springhill Miners' Museum explains how coal is mined and the dangers of the underground work.

(902) 592-3449
Open mid-May–mid-Oct.
daily, 9–5

Directions: Follow Route 2, 1 km (0.6 mi.) from Main Street. The museum is at 145 Black River Road. (Don't be fooled into driving toward the tower you see from the main road. You'll end up by a correctional centre with no one to give you directions.)

The Anne Murray Centre

One of the biggest music stars to come from Nova Scotia is Anne Murray. She grew up in Springhill, where her father was a doctor and where many members of her family still live. The Anne Murray Centre is a celebration of a hometown girl who made good.

The Anne Murray Centre is a fascinating tribute to one of Canada's most famous artists.

One of the fascinating things about the centre—like facilities dedicated to other famous people—is how many items from her youth are

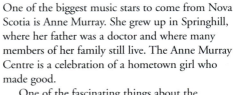

preserved. It's as if, knowing she would one day be famous, her mother never threw anything away. This collection contains early report cards, school clothes, toys, and her first contract with the CBC where she earned $71.50 a week, unless she performed solo, which bumped her pay up to $99 a week.

Throughout the centre are videos about Anne's life and accomplishments. Others feature a particular performance: with Glen Campbell, on Front Page Challenge, etc., and, of course, her music is heard from one display room to the next.

(902) 597-8614
Open mid-May–mid-Oct.
daily 9–5;
other times by chance or appointment

Anne Murray has been famous for so long that many of her fellow Bluenosers might still be surprised by the extent of her accomplishments. She's been on radio and television, performed in concert, released dozens of albums, and sold millions of records (don't miss the gold room!). On top of this, Murray has won just about every music award available.

For those who love reading other people's mail there's a case of correspondence from celebrities like Burt Reynolds and Doris Day.

It's impressive that someone from such a tiny community that has seen many hard times, could rise to Murray's level of success. Perhaps this should be a required stop for all students in the province.

It is an inspiring, rather than boastful, stop.

Directions: The centre is located at 36 Main Street in Springhill.

Fundy Geological Museum

Driving past Nova Scotia's fishing villages, farms, and forests it's easy to forget the importance of mining to the provincial economy. The wealth of commercial mineral deposits—salt, gold, gypsum, coal, amethyst, limestone, slate, marble, lead, tin, silver, copper, jasper, agate—belies the rich geological history of the province.

Nova Scotia has been a jungle, desert, swamp, sea floor, volcanic hotbed, and covered by kilometres-thick glaciers. As a result of all this climate and physical change, Nova Scotia is a wealth of fossils, minerals, and landforms, making the province a geologist's and palaeontologist's dream.

While the province doesn't unearth skeletal remains of the size featured in movies, Nova Scotia does have its own compact, equally nasty-looking prehistoric creatures. The Fundy Geological Museum explores provincial history through millions of years of geological activity.

Visitors can watch lab researchers work on new finds, study dioramas of some of the strange creatures which lived here before humans, and see 325 million-year-old fossils. Some of these fossils are so small it's a wonder anyone saw them which gives the museum an opportunity to explain how scientists see potential in a rock.

The museum also offers lots of great programs for kids, including gallery sleepovers, though they may not get much sleep among dinosaur replicas!

This is a relatively new museum, built to house the rapidly growing fossil collection and items unearthed across Nova Scotia, like mastodons. For those interested in landscape and life, geography and geological history, this is a must see.

Directions: In Parrsboro, turn at the old post office and war memorial, then turn right past a small lake. The museum is at 6 Two Islands Road.

The fossil-rich Fundy museum explores the province's geological history.

(902) 254-3814
Open year-round
June 1–Oct. 15
daily 9:30–5:30
Oct. 16–May 31
Tues.– Sat. 9–5

Age of Sail Heritage Centre

The Age of Sail Heritage Centre doesn't have a grand collection, but it does have a wonderful feel and amusing presentation making it well worth seeing.

Of all the buildings turned into museums and community centres, few have had the multiple history of this one. It began as the Methodist church, became a sail loft then a community centre, and was finally moved to its present site just north of the village to become a museum. It's located beside a tidal bay once used to launch ships manufactured here. Most Nova Scotians have never heard of Port Greville, but for one hundred years, four hundred ships were built and launched from here.

Located on an original shipbuilding site, the Age of Sail Heritage Centre highlights the industries that once thrived along the Minas Basin.

The museum's rarest item is a twenty-eight star American Flag. Use of this flag dates from July 4, 1846 to 1847. However, the museum's best features are a thirty-seven minute video showing life at sea, and a recreated kitchen. Even though the video was shot in 1929 by an American sailor, it is a wonderfully vivid, candid look at life on the sea. Part of the video shows an horrendous storm. The waves splashing across the deck are so thick they obliterate half the ship. The narrator, who happens to be the sailor who shot the film, tells the importance of keeping the hand-cranked foghorn in operation. Consequently, he says, "The stupidest man on the crew was given the task of operating the foghorn." To this day, whenever he hears a foghorn he thinks, "There's a fool fully employed."

The other fun exhibit is known as "Grannie." Activated by a sensor, Grannie sits in her rocker by the kitchen stove, speaking to anyone walking by. Her dialogue is that of many Grannies, maiden aunts, or "widowed women." It's amusing because it's a familiar cliché.

(902) 348-2060
or 348-2030
Open Victoria Day to Labour Day
Tues.–Sun. 10–6;
weekends and special tours until Thanksgiving;
other times by appointment

The Age of Heritage Centre also has a blacksmith shop, a charming little tea room, and a ten thousand name computerized genealogical centre.

Directions: Follow Route 209, north of the Village of Port Greville (between Parrsboro and Joggins).

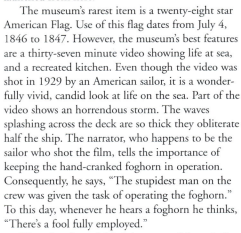

Showcase Nova Scotia

There's a mastodon on a ridge overlooking the Trans-Canada Highway between Truro and Halifax. This attention-getter draws travellers into the Showcase Nova Scotia site located at the convenience centre beside the highway. This may be an odd location for a museum/exhibition centre, but for people in a hurry it's a perfect, concise introduction to the province.

The facility has a series of high-tech capsules, starting with a Star Trek-like command console (kids will love it) explaining how the actual landmass of Nova Scotia was formed. The Age of the Mastodon exhibit contains a mural, mastodon bones, and a video about early plants and mammals.

The Settlers exhibit provokes a chuckle or two when the pioneer wife signs, "How sick I am of trees ..." There's also an Industry and Commerce exhibit, a Native People exhibit, and a Hidden Treasures section geared to children, who get to dig in a sandbox. Perhaps the best exhibit is the Halifax Explosion that features photographic enlargements of a streetscape, which rotates to show the area before and after the explosion.

Each small exhibit space is made up of artifacts, photographs, and an audio segment activated by sensors. For those passing through the province, the Showcase gives the historical highlights and ends with a ten minute video about Nova Scotia. For those who are on a leisurely schedule, it's like a hearty appetizer leading around the province. It's a good way to break up a long drive.

Directions: From the Trans-Canada Highway, take Exit 11. In Stewiacke, head for 87 Main Street West.

The mastodon is the landmark for Showcase Nova Scotia, a lively visual and audio exhibit that offers a concise introduction to the province.

(902) 639-2345
Open May–Dec.
summer hours 9:30–8
off-season 10–6

Lawrence House Museum

(902) 216-2628
Open June 1–Oct. 15
Mon.–Sat. 9:39–5:30
Sun. 1–5:30

Communities around the Minas Basin and Bay of Fundy prospered in the age of sail. Favoured with the world's highest tides, entrepreneurs were able to save money by building ships near the source of raw materials (the forests).

In this glory period, no one was more successful than Maitland builder than William D. Lawrence. In 1874 Lawrence launched the *WD Lawrence,* the largest sailing ship ever constructed in Canada. The jumbo jet of its day, the *WD Lawrence* weighed 2459 tonnes (2710 tons), was 80 m (262 ft.) long (four times the length of his museum), and had a 15 m (48 ft.) beam.

Inside Lawrence House there are formal parlours, dining room, bedrooms, kitchen, office, and the small room above the front hall, where Lawrence watched the events at his shipyard, all with their original furniture.

Equal to the stature of his ships is Lawrence House. Built across the road from his shipyard, the house museum has twenty rooms open to the public.

The first thing to notice about the house is the shipwright's influence on the front steps. They are modelled after those to a ship's bridge. Likewise, the interior stairway resembles those found below decks. The kitchen and pantry cupboards also show a shipbuilder's sensibility for order and economy of space.

Interestingly, this is one of the few mansion museums to have any type of indoor plumbing. The house's lone bathroom, beyond the kitchen, consists of a sink, pump, and built-in tin tub. In what is laughable luxury now, Lawrence had two two-seat privies connected to the back of the house via a covered walkway.

W. D. Lawrence was an inquisitive, self-confident early entrepreneur, who believed that "Labour is the genius that changes forests into ships, and ugliness into beauty.... There is nothing better than sharp opposition to make a man succeed in his business."

W. D. Lawrence lived a successful life, and his home shows it.

Directions: In Maitland follow Route 215 (the main road through the community). Follow the key signs. The museum is easily found.

Sunrise Trail

27 Cumberland County Museum
28 Sutherland Steam Mill Museum
29 Balmoral Grist Mill Museum
30 Hector Heritage Quay, McCulloch House Museum, and Hector Exhibit and Research Centre
31 Sobey Collection of Canadian Art
32 Nova Scotia Museum of Industry

Cumberland County Museum

Geographically, the Cumberland County Museum in Amherst is the first museum in Nova Scotia. It is located in Grove Cottage, the former home of Robert B. Dickey, a Father of Confederation.

The museum has a small collection of artifacts heavily weighted toward natural resources—mining has been a leading industry in this region. An unexpected part of the collection is a display of prisoner-of-war arts and crafts. Prisoners with time on their hands used to occupy themselves by carving left-

over soup bones and bits of wood, or by working in leather—anything to keep busy and bring in cash. It's a tradition going back to Napoleonic times, when French prisoners supplemented their diet by selling similar items. The items in this display were made at an interment camp in Amherst during the First World War; it is a rarity among provincial collections.

The museum also acts as the local cultural centre and has a gallery for travelling and local art exhibitions. Upstairs there is an extensive archives on Acadian and Yorkshire immigration.

Directions: The museum is at 150 Church Street in Amherst.

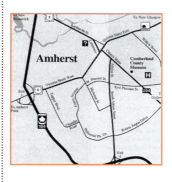

The handicrafts of prisoners of war are a unique aspect of the collection here.

(902) 667-2561
Open June 1–
Labour Day
Mon.–Sat. 9–5
Sun. 2–5
Labour Day–Dec. 1
Tues.–Sat. 10–4
Dec. 1–Mar. 1
Wed.–Sat. 10–4
Mar. 31–June 1
Tues.–Sat. 10–4

Sutherland Steam Mill Museum

The Sutherland Steam Mill Museum is an illustration of basic business principles: take an abundant resource (wood), use skilled labour to add value and take advantage of the proximity to cheap transportation to ship products to market. The area around the Sutherland Steam Mill had all these elements: lumber, labour and railway connections.

Today it's difficult to believe that this weathered building was ever "modern." When it was built in 1894, the Sutherland Steam Mill employed the new technology of the day: steam power.

The mill's innovation took shape in a variety of unusual forms, like the early sprinkler system. Fire was always a concern, especially in a mill with sawdust and wood shavings under hot saws. As a preventative measure, the mill owners lined up six rain barrels along the roof ridge to help fight any fire. Another innovation was the pragmatic frugality of moving the family bathtub into the mill to thaw frozen wood shingles.

Operated until 1958, the Sutherland Steam Mill's primary products were sleighs, carriages, sleds, building materials and housing trim. The Victorians' love of ornate "gingerbread" decorated homes created a steady demand for the Sutherland's products.

Upstairs, half-finished work hangs from the rafters, and rocking horses sit on the workbenches as if waiting for Christmas.

Phone for details on the monthly fire-up day, when steam hisses, belts slap and equipment thunders.

Steam allowed production to increase as much as twenty times over the water-powered standards in the 1890s.

(902) 657-3365
or 657-3016
Open June 1–Oct. 15
Mon.–Sat. 9:30–5:30
Sun. 1–5:30

Directions: Take Highway 326 to Denmark, near Tatamagouche. Follow the blue key signs.

Balmoral Grist Mill Museum

Travelling through the province's museum sites, one notices how many items were made in Nova Scotia. We built clocks, cars, stoves, furniture, ships, we made our own clothing, and grew our own food. We were incredibly self-sufficient.

One area of self-sufficiency—food—was enhanced by the proliferation of local mills. The Balmoral Grist Mill situated on Matheson's Brook, is the last of four hundred grist mills which operated in Nova Scotia. The mill is nestled in a park-like forest setting, beside a man-made pond where fish sometimes jump out of the water. It is a lovely, tranquil area.

Grain is ground here today as it was in 1874.

Grinding grain is a fairly dull process until guides explain the different grinding stones and grains and why each one is needed. A tour of the three-level mill gives an appreciation for today's convenience. In the days when residents relied on a grist mill, it could take two and a half days to make oatmeal!

Four times daily the operation is "fired up" for a milling demonstration. The place comes alive with grinding mill stones, creaking wooden gears, and taught ropes shaking with tension as they pass from floor to floor. At times the mill shakes and shudders so it feels as it might below deck on a ship. Then the mill fills with a fine cloud of dust.

There is a natural poetry to the grist mill. Maybe because it is made entirely from the land—wood, stone, and water—that it is so comfortable, cozy, and friendly.

Freshly milled flour is sold in the museum gift shop.

(902) 657-3016
Open: June 1–Oct. 15
Mon.–Sat. 9:30–5:30
Sun. 1–5:30

Directions: Off Route 311 on Highway 256, follow signs to Balmoral Grist Mill, which is near Tatamagouche.

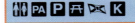

Hector Heritage Quay, McCulloch House Museum, and Hector Exhibit and Research Centre

Scottish heritage dominates Pictou's architecture, activities, tastes, and history. The three main Celtic landmarks are the Hector Heritage Quay, McCulloch House, and Hector Exhibit and Research Centre.

The *Hector* brought Scottish immigrants to "New Scotland" (Nova Scotia is Latin for New Scotland), after their defeat at the Battle of Culloden in 1746. Desperate for a new life, away from their English victors, these Scots boarded ships for the false promise of the new world. Although they were ill-equipped to meet the challenges of a hostile and untamed environment, their stoicism saw them through.

McCulloch House was built in 1806.

Hector Heritage Quay is a museum and interpretation centre devoted to the twenty thousand Scots who left their homeland between 1763 and 1777. In addition to the heritage centre, a full-scale replica of the *Hector* is also being built on the grounds. Visitors are free to wander on board and experience the stifling below-deck existence immigrants experienced crossing the Atlantic.

See the *Hector* at Hector Heritage Quay.

Across town, the McCulloch House Museum was the home of the Rev. Thomas McCulloch, a Presbyterian minister, physician, and "learned man." A visionary with modern controversial ideas, McCulloch believed in universal education. He established Pictou Academy and was the first president of what is now Dalhousie University.

Down the hill form McCulloch House is the Hector Exhibit and Research Centre. It is a multi-purpose facility which contains an archive, genealogical centre and exhibition space for art shows.

These three facilities work together to tell the story of Scottish immigration.

Hector Centre has a large genealogy collection.

Directions: Hector Heritage Quay is at 33 Caladh Avenue in Pictou. Restaurants are nearby. McCulloch House is located at 100 Haliburton Road. The Hector Exhibition and Research Centre is at 86 Old Haliburton Road.

Hector Heritage Quay:
(902) 485-4371/8028
Open mid-May–mid-Oct. 9–9 daily
McCulloch House:
(902) 485-1150
Open June 1–Oct. 15
Mon.–Sat. 9:30–5:30
Sun. 1–5:30
Hector Centre
(902) 485-1150
Open year-round
Wed.–Sat. 9:30–5:30
Sun. 1–5:30

McCulloch:
Hector Quay:
Hector Centre:

31 Sobey Collection of Canadian Art

The Sobey Collection of Canadian Art is a an absolute joy to discover; it's like an abbreviated visit to the National Gallery in Ottawa.

The patriarch of the family grocery business, Frank Sobey, used his success to indulge a passion for Canadian paintings. His collection is now housed in Crombie House, a riverside estate on the road between Pictou and New Glasgow.

The collection and estate are open to the public every Wednesday in July and August. There are eighty-eight canvases in the collection. The tour is guided and takes fifty-five minutes—and is an absolute must see.

This collection is a conjugation of nineteenth and twentieth century Canadian masterpieces. It includes twelve works by Krieghoff, four by Lauren Harris, and three by Emily Carr. There are three Tom Thomsons in the dining room alone, and the entire Group of Seven is represented in the living room.

Equally fascinating is the humour and knowledge of the guide, who talks about Emily Carr's poverty (Carr was so poor she mixed house paint with gas), explains the light in Thomson's work, and follows the evolution from the greeting card style of the Montreal School of painting to the revolutionary Group of Seven. It's an enriching, fun, fascinating, and never dull tour.

Directions: Follow the Sunrise Trail between Pictou and New Glasgow. The Sobey Collection is at 1780 Abercrombie Road, New Glasgow. Signage is sparse, so keep a lookout.

(902) 755-4440, ext. 3439 or 752-6016
Open Wed. in July and August.
Guided tours at 9, 10, 11 A.M., and 1, 2, 3 and 4 P.M.

Nova Scotia Museum of Industry

Traditionally, history has focused on the well-born, the famous, the powerful: aristocrats, judges, writers, inventors, adventurers and generals. But increasingly, history is looking at the lives and lifestyles of workers. The Nova Scotia Museum of Industry tells the story of "the people whose stories were not recorded, but whose lives and work are still important."

This is a fascinating collection, in Atlantic Canada's largest museum, of lifestyle and industrial artifacts. The museum not only explains how and why the province was developed, it shows how technology brought lower-cost products or labour-saving devices into the home from the workplace.

One of many highlights here are the two oldest steam locomotives in North America.

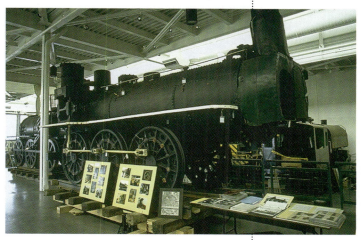

The museum uses a number of interactive displays to demonstrate how hard work contributes to invention. For instance, lifting a shadow item intended to duplicate a kettle's weight illustrates that housework wasn't for wimps.

A simulated mine shaft shows how early miners laid on their sides in coffin-sized crawl spaces, picking away at the coal seam. The Industrial Revolution relied on men, machines, and coal—the black mineral which has played such a significant role in Nova Scotia's economy. Upstairs, in the museum the coal industry's toll is commemorated in displays and honour rolls from all the province's mining disasters, including the May 9, 1992, Westray explosion which killed twenty-six men.

The McKay car history began in Kentville in 1910.

The mining displays illustrate the power that mine managers and companies exercised over miners and their families. Perhaps this is a museum at its most successful.

The main artifact to see is *Sampson,* an 1838 steam locomotive used in the Albion Mines. The oldest steam engine in Canada, it weighs 18 tons (16 tonnes), had a maximum speed of 8 mph (13 km/hr) and was stoked from the front.

The rest of the collection is as diverse as it is interesting, ranging from the collapsible furniture designed and built in Nova Scotia, to grand touring cars, to familiar household items from the thirties through to the sixties.

This refreshingly different collection forms one of the best museums in the province. It will appeal to young and old, inventor and entrepreneur.

(902) 755-5425
Open year-round
Summer Mon.–Sat.
9–5:30
Sun. 10–5
Winter Mon.–Sat.
9:30–5
Sun. 1–5

Directions: Take Exit 24 from the Trans-Canada Highway 104. The museum is located at 147 North Foord Street in Stellarton.

Discover Nova Scotia Museums and Art Galleries

Cape Breton Trails

- **Cabot Trail**
33 Alexander Graham Bell National Historic Site
34 Margaree Salmon Museum
35 Les Trois Pignons/ Elizabeth LeFort Gallery
36 Great Hall of the Clans

- **Bras d'Or Lakes Scenic Drive**
37 Nova Scotia Highland Village
38 Orangedale Railway Station Museum

- **Fleur-de-lis Trail, Marconi Trail & Metro Cape Breton**
39 Fortress of Louisbourg National Historic Site
40 Sydney and Louisbourg Railway Museum
41 Glace Bay Miner's Museum
42 Marconi National Historic Site
43 Jost House Museum, Cossit House Museum, St. Patrick's Church Museum and the Lyceum
44 University College of Cape Breton Art Gallery

33 Alexander Graham Bell National Historic Site

One man, so many ideas is, perhaps, the best synopsis of the Bell Museum.

The Alexander Graham Bell Museum is in Baddeck because Bell so loved the area he spent thirty-seven summers here on his estate called Beinn Bhreagh (Gaelic for "beautiful mountain"). Bell summed up his feelings with the observation, "I have travelled around the globe. I have seen the Canadian and American Rockies, the Andes, the Alps and the Highlands of Scotland, but for simple beauty Cape Breton out-rivals them all."

The Alexander Graham Bell National Historic Site looks at all aspects of the man: inventor, teacher, husband, parent, and grandfather.

The museum attempts to cover all of Bell's many interests: the telephone, aviation, and teaching the deaf. Rather fittingly, the museum marries technology with history to show the scope of Bell's prodigious life. Five videos cover everything from his life in old newsreels, to the remembrances of relatives and estate workers. On video, Bell's daughters recollect with fondness how Bell always sat across from his wife Mabel, who was deaf, so she could read his lips, how he built a kite so big it lifted him off the ground, and how much he loved the Cape Breton countryside. The museum depicts a slightly eccentric, inquisitive and contemplative man who would roam the estate at night in his bathing suit "exploring the riddles of nature."

A computer display allows visitors to search a database, calling up pages from his many notebooks. The photo collection includes hundreds of shots of daily life at Beinn Bhreagh: flying kites with Helen Keller, conducting experiments, and walking hand-in-hand with Mabel down a country lane.

The museum is packed with memorabilia and scientific artifacts, including the original HD-4 hydrofoil. The Bell Museum catalogues genius but also manages to humanize the great inventor showing us his foibles and lust for life, his passion for Mabel, and his fear that friends would think him a one-hit wonder. Bell is quoted as saying, "I can't bear to hear that even my friends should think that I stumbled upon an invention and that there is no more good in me."

The museum is a major Canadian collection and should not be missed. A trip to Cape Breton is incomplete without seeing it.

The museum is an inspiring collection of prodigious work. Across the bay from the museum site is Bell's beloved and romantic Beinn Breagh.

Directions: Baddeck, on the Cabot Trail is located on Route 205 and Trans-Canada Highway 105. The Bell Museum is at 559 Chebucto Street.

(902) 295-2069
Admission charged
May 15–Oct. 15.
Open year-round
Winter daily 9–5
June & Sept. 9–7
July & Aug. 9–8

34 Margaree Salmon Museum

The Margaree is famous for fiddlers and fish. While there's no museum–yet–for fiddlers, there is one which celebrates fishing. The Margaree Salmon Museum is a pretty, well-kept building hidden under a canopy of thick maples in North East Margaree. For those who fish, you can't miss this museum. For those who don't, you'll be surprised by how much there is to know about fishing.

Fish are as much a part of the museum as fishing.

The Salmon Museum promotes the pleasures of angling, while reminding people of their responsibility for conservation of the stock and preservation of the river. The collection is amazing and exhaustive. There are books, videos, paintings, magazines, rods, reels, nets, and flies. Flies range from the 1860 Silver Doctor to the Free Trade Fly which has the Canadian flag on one side and the U.S. Stars and Stripes on the other.

The museum promotes the pleasures of angling.

While fishing may seem such a straightforward pastime—toss a line in a river and wait for a bite—the guide, who admits she "has been known to wet a line herself," explains the development of hooks (before 1880 they had no eyes) and reels and the evolution of fishing rods. A wall of rods shows exotic combinations of style and material like rock maple, split cane, ash, and early rods which rested on the hip. Even fishing lines have history. They have been made of gut, horsehair, silk, and enamel.

(902) 248-2848
Open June 15–
Oct. 15
daily 9–5

The collection includes some taxidermy, a so-called bad boys' (poachers) corner, and displays on the life cycle of salmon and trout.

Although a single-subject museum can become tiresome for anyone but the passionate fanatic, the Margaree Salmon Museum is just the right size to interest everyone from fanatic, environmentalist, conservationist, to casual observer. It's well thought out, focused, and interesting.

Directions: Take Exit 7 from the Trans-Canada Highway to North East Margaree, on the Cabot Trail. Watch for signs leading the way to the museum.

Les Trois Pignons/Elizabeth LeFort Gallery

Chéticamp is a brightly-coloured Acadian community gripping the Gulf of St. Lawrence shore on Cape Breton Island.

Surrounded by a sea of Scots, Chéticamp is a bastion of Acadian culture. Les Trois Pignons/ Elizabeth LeFort Gallery at the northern end of the village contains a genealogical centre, library, gallery and museum.

The LeFort Gallery celebrates the artistry of Dr. Elizabeth LeFort and the women of Chéticamp. The community is famous for rug hooking and tapestries. As visitors travel throughout Nova Scotia's historic houses, Chéticamp hooked rugs are found everywhere. While many Chéticamp women have hooked rugs, Dr. LeFort is probably the best known practitioner of this art form. Her work hangs in Buckingham Palace, the White House, the Vatican, and Rideau Hall.

Twenty-two of her works hang in the local gallery. These hooked rugs are surprising, looking more like paintings than bits of wool painstakingly pulled through a backing to create wonderfully " textured images.

In addition to the gallery of hooked rugs and tapestries, there is a museum, Les Trois Pignons, which is the life's work of another Chéticamp woman. The museum's collection consists mostly of decorative arts, including old examples of Chéticamp rugs.

Hooking demonstrations take place throughout the season.

Directions: Follow the Cabot Trail to Chéticamp. The museum/gallery is at 15584 Main Street.

Chéticamp is renowned for the artistry of rug hooking and tapestries. Born in the village, Catherine Poirier's hooked rugs have a charming quality.

(902) 224-2612 or 224-2642
Open mid–May–Oct. 31 9–5
July & Aug. 9–8

36 Great Hall of the Clans, The Gaelic College

The Great Hall of the Clans located on the grounds of the Gaelic College in South Gut, St. Ann's, is like a parade of tartans. Lining the sides of the hall are stone supports encasing twelve clan displays. Each display includes family history, heraldic details, and clan apparel: kilts, trousers, capes, and gowns.

The Great Hall also contains Scottish ancestral heritage, armorial explanations, and reams of fascinating details about clans. The collection includes such information as a history of tartan, the pattern stick, and the kilt's original purpose.

Just outside the Great Hall is a small museum about Scottish immigration and migration. This area around St. Ann's was originally settled by Sutherlandshire Scots in 1817. But in 1851, eight hundred residents moved to New Zealand. The museum traces this movement and the development of parallel communities. There is even a small gallery which features a collection of paintings about the move to New Zealand, the farewell, and the new life.

The college is like a summer school for Celtic arts and is unique in North America. It has piping and fiddle schools, residences, a gift shop, practice facilities, classrooms, and a cafeteria.

If you're itching to practice Gaelic, this is the stop to make.

Trace Gaelic ancestry and clan systems at the Great Hall. Local history and artwork are also highlighted.

(902) 295-3411
Open June 15–Oct. 15
daily 8:30–5

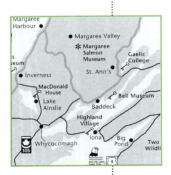

Directions: Take Exit 11 of the Trans-Canada Highway 105. Head for the Nova Scotia Gaelic College of Arts and Culture in South Gut St. Ann's. The college is 0.4 km (1/4 mi.) off the highway.

Discover Nova Scotia Museums and Art Galleries

Nova Scotia Highland Village

The Highland Village in Iona is not to be overlooked. For those who may be weary of gazing at artifacts this 17 ha (43 acre) site offers striking views, situated on a hillside overlooking the Bras d'Or Lakes.

Like Sherbrooke Village on the Marine Drive, this is a living history museum with an exclusively Highland Scots focus. The Highland Village traces Scottish immigration and the evolution of their society in New Scotland (Nova Scotia). A tour begins in a small stone-and-sod hut called the Black House. Today this would be viewed as a primitive barn, but for many highlanders this shieling was home. Although this type of building was never used in North America, it illustrates what the Scots were leaving behind. Up the hill is the log cabin, an example of the Scots' first dwelling in their new land.

The village illustrates a subtle evolutionary progression in accommodation and lifestyle, from heating and cooking over open fires to the development of stoves, which allowed residents to built larger, more comfortable homes.

The wood stove (top) was an innovation that allowed the Scots to build larger homes like the 1875–1900 period home, above.

There are ten buildings in the village. Each is furnished according to its period and purpose. There is also a barn, blacksmith's shop, one-room schoolhouse, general store and a carding mill, all components of an early Highland Scots village to create an authentic setting.

The collection includes a black-and-chrome, horse-drawn hearse, complete with grey tassels and trim (last used in 1942), an old telephone exchange, Alexander Graham Bell's bright yellow carriage with blue seats, and the obligatory long-horned highland cattle grazing behind the schoolhouse. In light of Canada's ongoing constitutional discussions, there's a fascinating 1907 map of the Dominion in the school, which shows vastly different borders for the Province of Quebec.

Since the village focuses on living history, be

In a picturesque setting, Iona Village historic homes reveal that many immigrants did well to survive the harsh winters.

prepared to see work in progress: the blacksmith at the forge, women baking on open hearths, weaving, or taking part in a milling frolic. Many of these handmade items are sold at the general store.

This museum spans 180 years of settlement—a great place to learn about history by seeing it in action. Although the Highland Village may be off the beaten path, it shouldn't be off a list of places to see. There is a restaurant and motel next door.

Directions: Take Exit 6 off the Trans-Canada Highway 105. Proceed 19 km (12 mi.) east toward Iona. The Highland Village is on Route 223 at 4119 in Iona.

(902) 725-2272
Open June 1–Oct. 5
Mon.–Sat. 9–5
Sun. 10–6

Orangedale Railway Station Museum

Many people are familiar with the Rankin Family song "Orangedale Whistle," which is about this very railway. The village of Orangedale was once a transportation hub funnelling rail traffic between Baddeck, Sydney, Glace Bay, Louisbourg, the Cabot Trail, and mainland Nova Scotia. The nineteenth-century station used to serve six passenger and twenty freight trains daily. It ceased operation in 1990.

The museum shows how the station looked and worked in its heyday. In theatrical terms it gives a front-of and back-of the house look at station operations. One waiting room and ticket office remain intact (the former "Ladies Waiting Room" holds another railway exhibit). The hardwood benches, brass ticket cage and pot-bellied stove embody a universal image of travel in Canada, especially in winter.

The stationmaster's office is filled with paperwork and signal switches as it was when this was a working station. Upstairs the stationmaster's apartment is open, showing how he and his family lived, sometimes sharing their home with stranded travellers.

The museum collection also includes several pieces of rolling stock. There's a massive snow plow with a surprisingly simple dash, considering how big and powerful the vehicle is, and a caboose among a few other railway cars.

The museum answers questions visitors may not know they had: how did the stationmaster live, and what could conductors and drivers see as they rolled across the countryside?

Directions: From Trans-Canada Highway 105, take Exit 4. Follow the southern loop of the Bras d'Or Lakes Scenic Drive to Orangedale. The museum is located at 1428 Orangedale Road in the village of Orangedale.

In its heyday, Cape Bretoners would come to Orangedale by horse, by carriage, on foot and, later, by vehicle to catch trains to the rest of Canada.

(902) 756-3384
Open June 1–Sept. 30
Mon.–Sat. 10–6
Sun. 1–6
or by appointment

Fortress Louisbourg National Historic Site

The Fortress of Louisbourg has always been described with superlatives. When the original fortress was under construction, it was so large and so expensive that even the spendthrift Louis XV complained, "I half expect to rise from my bed in Versailles and one day see the towers of Louisbourg rising over the horizon." The king, in what he thought was an economy measure, banned all lawyers from Louisbourg. Civil servants took their place and buried everyone in paperwork—so far researchers have uncovered 850,000 documents.

Parks Canada has restored only a fraction of the eighteenth-century town; the present fortress is the largest historic restoration in North America. It comprises fifty buildings, and covers 5 ha (12 acres) so don't expect to see it all in an hour. Come prepared with comfortable walking shoes and extra layers of clothing for changeable weather. It's usually cooler at the fortress than in the town of Louisbourg.

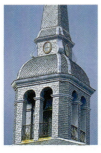

Within the town walls, Louisbourg has its own church.

Sentries and town patrol are seen "on duty" around the grounds.

Louisbourg was built for two reasons. First was the abundance of fish off Nova Scotia which served the enormous demand for fish created by Catholic Europe's meatless Fridays. France, to protect access to the fishing grounds, felt the need for a fortress and naval base nearby. Second, by strategically positioning a fortress at Louisbourg the French could control access to the Gulf of St. Lawrence and protect their Quebec colony.

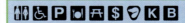

In the early 1700s Louisbourg seemed impenetrable. Its power and size unnerved the English colonists along the Eastern Seaboard, who lived in uneasy coexistence with the French. In 1744 the French at Louisbourg learned of war between England and France before the other colonies, and attacked and destroyed Canso. New Englanders who lost family, friends, and business interests responded by launching an invasion of Louisbourg the following year. This was the first of two great sieges at Louisbourg.

Three years after the first seige, Louisbourg was returned to the French. Colonists lived in relative peace until 1758 when it was again captured and destroyed by the British.

In its non-combative days, Louisbourg lived the life of a French city. The poor and military were cold, rough and rowdy. The elite lead a cultured life attending balls, dinner parties, and parlour games in rooms as elegant as any chateau in France. This is what makes Louisbourg so interesting—it is a complete microcosm of French society.

The Louisbourg of today shows all aspects of life, from the garrison's barracks, to warehouses, shops and taverns, to merchant homes, the church, to the governor's apartments in the King's Bastion. Walking the streets of the site is like being transported to eighteenth century France. The buildings are made of stone. Members of the Compagnies Franches de la Marine patrol the parapets. And costumed citizens go about daily life as if it were 1744. Children play, housewives gossip on the streets, the bread man sells warm loaves from a basket strapped to his back, ladies entertain in their salons, and cooks toil by the heat of open fires.

Fortress Louisbourg is animated by workers in period costume to portray eighteenth-century life within the fortress.

One of the most spectacular fireworks displays in the province is held on Fête de St. Louis (the Sunday closest to August 25), when an attack is recreated as part of the festival.

Fortress Louisbourg is one of the most impressive historic sites in Canada—well worth superlatives!

The drummers wore brightly coloured costumes to be the most easily recognized among military members.

(902) 733-2280
Open June 1–
Oct. 12
daily 9:30–5;
July & Aug. 9–7;
in May there are guided tours only;
Oct 12–30 grounds are open but not buildings.

Directions: The Louisbourg site is located 35 km (22 mi.) south of Sydney.

Discover
Nova Scotia
Museums and
Art Galleries

Sydney and Louisbourg Railway Museum

Everything about the coal mining industry is heavy. The equipment is heavy, the risk is heavy, the darkness is heavy and the product (coal) is heavy. Transporting coal has always been done on carts of some sort, whether man-powered, horse-drawn, or engine-driven.

This need to move heavy loads created the demand for rail lines in Cape Breton in the early 1800s. Over the decades, Louisbourg became a major port —shipping coal from thirty island mines around the world. The company that moved the coal was the Sydney and Louisbourg Railway. The S&L Railway is gone now, but its former station, rolling stock, and equipment form the nucleus of the museum collection.

The museum is full of tools used to keep a railway running. Railways, like the huge engines which pull the trains, require hard labour to operate. The scale of everything is huge. The train lights could substitute for lighthouses, and the oil cans look as if they would take two men to lift. Of course, they didn't, but working with objects like this would certainly eliminate any need to go to a gym.

Outside, the museum displays several pieces of rolling stock. Especially interesting are the Pullman cars. These cars show the development of personal travel and explain why people always felt the need to rest after their journey. Inside, the surprisingly tall cars are painted in inventive colour schemes—red, green, yellow, and brown. One car has a hand pump and sink for the travellers' convenience. Another has a private compartment with frosted glass, brass rails, plush seating, and private washroom.

If you're in Louisbourg, take a few minutes to see this interesting collection.

Directions: The museum is at 7336 Main Street in Louisbourg (on the main road from Sydney).

The Sydney and Louisbourg Railway once carried coal to port from thirty Cape Breton mines.

(902) 733-2720
Open mid-May–mid-Oct
May–June, Sept. & Oct. 9–5
July & Aug. 8–8

41 Glace Bay Miner's Museum

Anyone who has ever questioned their working conditions should visit the Glace Bay Miner's Museum. This area of Cape Breton has been mined since 1720 when coal was first used to heat

Louisbourg. Mining was considered a good job for young men, who quickly aged in the unforgiving environment of early mines.

Part of the museum experience is a mine tour. Visitors are outfitted in hard hats and capes, then treated to an explanation on how mines are dug, safety procedures (for working mines) and candid, sometimes shocking details of the miner's daily routine. For instance, after a sweaty shift below ground, the miners returned topside, showered and hung their work clothes on hooks which were hoisted up to the ceiling to dry. The miners wore these same clothes day after day until they took their vacation. Only then did the work clothes go home to be washed!

The mine shaft is a head-hitting five feet high and most people explore it half bent over. After the mine, visitors slip into a simulated model train, once used to take miners to the work site, to view a video. It's great fun for kids because the cars jiggle along with the film. Wear sensible shoes, something with a good tread, as the mine floor is slippery.

There's also an above ground museum, plus a small miner's village which shows how the miner's family lived. They were in essence, indentured serfs. They worked for the company, lived in company houses, and shopped at the company store. If they lost their job, they lost everything: income, home, and credit. The museum is a stark place which speaks of past sacrifices of a brutal life.

Directions: The museum is located at Quarry Point 42 Birkley Street (off South Street) in Glace Bay. (Look for the black signs—it's easily found). Food is available at the museum in the summer.

The Glace Bay Miners' Museum takes a candid look at coal mining practices. Retired miners give guided tours of Ocean Deeps Colliery.

(902) 849-4522
Open year-round
June 3–Aug. 31,
daily 10–6
Tues. until 7;
Sept. 2–May 3,
Mon.–Fri. 9–4

Marconi National Historic Site

At the beginning of the twentieth century on a cliff overlooking the Atlantic Ocean, the breakthrough in modern communications took place. It was from this barren end of Glace Bay, called Table Head, that Italian inventor Guglielmo Marconi sent the first wireless message across the Atlantic Ocean.

Marconi established his wireless facility here because of Cape Breton Island's then-booming economy, and because Alexander Graham Bell had a home on the island. The so-called "Wizard of the Wireless" worked at the Bell laboratories in Baddeck to make his vision to "girdle the earth" with wireless communications a reality.

Learn about Marconi's innovation in wireless communication.

In an age of palm-sized technology that can transmit documents anywhere on the globe, Marconi's clunky and easily disrupted technology seems incredibly naive. But it was cutting edge enough to win him the Nobel Prize for Physics in 1909. And it was thanks to Marconi's wireless that anyone survived the *Titanic* disaster.

(902) 295-2069 or 842-2530 (summer only)
Open June 1–Oct. 15 daily 10–6

Today these events are preserved at the Marconi National Historic Site. Parks Canada has built an "interpretation centre" at Table Head. There are a few artifacts, but the centre's focus is more on a video, quotations, illustrations and explanations of Marconi's invention and his life. This can be an amusing stop for the generally inquisitive, shortwave afficionadoes and those with a penchant for inventions or technology.

Every April 25th—Marconi's birthday—the Sydney Amateur Radio Club celebrates by broadcasting from Table Head. Their call letters are VAS: Voice of the Atlantic Seaboard.

Directions: The museum is located on Timmerman Street at Table Head in Glace Bay. The Hub ballfields are opposite Timmerman Street, where visitors turn right for the Marconi Site. It can be tricky to find.

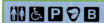

43 Jost House Museum, Cossit House Museum, St. Patrick's Church Museum and the Lyceum

Sydney is the unofficial capital of Cape Breton. Now part of "industrial Cape Breton" the Sydney area has always been known for coal mining, out of which grew supporting industries, such as a steel foundry and heavy manufacturing.

Sydney's first settlers were not Scots but United Empire Loyalists who came from New York in 1785. Scottish immigration did not start until twenty years later. The community's history is recounted in four facilities. The Jost House Museum shows the evolution of a family home from 1785 to 1900. The Jost family wasn't wealthy, but they were comfortably well-off. One of the more noticeable features of the house is the scale of furniture and ceilings. Everything is smaller, which reflects the stature of people in the eighteenth and nineteenth centuries—men were five feet two inches tall on average, and women four feet ten inches. So, watch your head.

The scale of the furnishings is noticeably smaller in Jost House because the stature of people was smaller in this period.

Upstairs the collections include a christening shawl given to a Sydney woman by Queen Victoria, an apothecary shop, and a display about the Second World War's impact on Sydney. It's easy to forget that Sydney, like other coastal communities, was on the front lines: 137 people died in 1942 when a U-boat sunk a Newfoundland-bound ferry.

Across the street is the oldest house in Sydney, the Cossit House Museum. It was built in 1787 by a proper, yet meddlesome Protestant minister, Ranna Cossit. Cossit was an early activist, who ignored the separation of Church and State, and involved himself in social, political, and education issues. He was so controversial that he was eventually transferred to Yarmouth.

Cossit House was home to the controversial Ranna Cossit and his wife and ten children.

Cossit House is an architecturally pure building. The house illustrates the austere, yet elegant life of a parsimonious cleric. The rooms are rich in colour, spare in furniture, but with ten Cossit children, floor space would still be at a premium.

One of the prize possessions at this museum is

Cossit:	👥 K 🏳
Jost:	👥 K B N
St. Patrick's:	👥 K N
Lyceum:	👥 ♿ N K

Cossit's letter book in which he meticulously copied over the contents of all letters he sent and received.

One street over from these two museum sites is St. Patrick's Church Museum—the oldest Roman Catholic church in Cape Breton. This 1828 church offers an intimate look at the larger community. It's a lovely post-and-beam, Gothic style building. Inside, the collection ranges from religious objects to lifestyle items to Admiral Parry's telescope, and there's a display on Moxham's Castle, a thirty room estate which used to exist in Sydney.

A short drive away is the Lyceum, which is the centre for arts and cultural groups in Sydney. In addition to a large gift shop there is meeting space and exhibition area. The Lyceum also houses the Cape Breton Centre for Heritage and Science, reading room, and a craft school.

St. Patrick's Church Museum's wide ranging collection offers insight into community life.

Directions: There is street parking only at each site. Cossit House is at 75 Charlotte Street in Sydney. Jost House is across the street at 54 Charlotte Street. St. Patrick's Church Museum is located at 87 Esplanade. The Lyceum is at 225 George Street, also in Sydney.

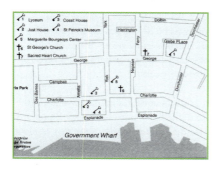

Cossit: (902) 539-7973
Open June 1–Oct. 15
Mon.–Sat. 9:30–5:30
Sun. 1–5:30
Jost: (902) 539-0366/1572
Open June 1–Oct. 31
Mon.–Sat. 9:30–5:30
Closed Sunday
Sept. & Oct.
Mon.–Sat. 10-4
St. Patrick's:
(902) 562-8237 or 539-1572
Open June 1–Labour Day, Mon.–Sat. 9:30–5:30
Sun. 1–5:30;
or by appointment
The Lyceum:
In summer Mon.–Sat. 9:30–5:30
In winter
Tues.–Fri. 10-4,
Sat. 1-4

University College of Cape Breton Art Gallery

44

The University College of Cape Breton (UCCB) Art Gallery is one of the few university galleries to regularly exhibit shows using their permanent collection. Perhaps this is because UCCB's collection is one of the largest in Eastern Canada.

Interestingly, in this Celtic heartland, where one expects to be inundated with plaid, UCCB has a large collection of contemporary art, including thirty serigraphs by Alex Colville.

The centrepiece of the collection is a Picasso sketchbook. A recent gift to the art gallery, the eighty-eight page book contains forty-four pen and ink sketches done by the artist between 1897 and 1902. Because of its value, the sketchbook is usually kept in a vault. However, it is periodically displayed in the gallery. Watch for notices or contact the gallery: by telephone (902) 563-1342, fax 563-1449, or e-mail bdavis@uccb.ns.ca.

The UCCB's gallery hosts in-house shows, exhibitions by Cape Breton artists, and travelling exhibitions. Their original gallery is dedicated to exhibits of local artists and artisans. Shows change every four to five weeks.

The UCCB Art Gallery collection includes contemporary works by such artists as Alex Colville.

Open year-round Mon.–Fri. 9–5; closed holidays; weekends by appointment

Directions: From Grand Lake Road, Sydney, turn right at the traffic lights onto University Boulevard and head for the main entrance in the new Student, Culture and Heritage Centre. The art gallery is the first door on the right.

Marine Drive

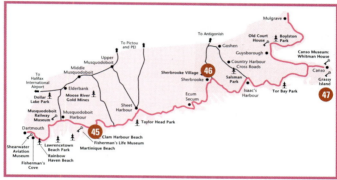

45 Fishermen's Life Museum
46 Sherbrooke Village
47 Canso Museum and Grassy Island National Historic Site

45 Fisherman's Life Museum

Humble and modest are apt descriptions for the Fisherman's Life Museum. The tiny, tidy home illustrates the dignity of work and the true meaning of family values.

The museum depicts one fisherman's family life, circa 1900. The James Myers family tale is an extraordinary one of hard work, dedication, and support. The twice-married Myers raised thirteen children in this house. And as meagre as Myers' income was from dory fishing, farming, and cooking at a lumber camp in winter, his children were all educated. In a period when women were not given educational opportunities, his daughters became secretaries, teachers, and nurses.

When one daughter contracted tuberculosis, Myers added a small, bright bedroom to the first floor so she could be cared for at home. She spent eighteen months segregated by a door from the family, seeing only her father and doctor.

The house is a testament to the harsh way of life for many Nova Scotia families. This is a prime example of the philosophy of "waste not, want not." In the kitchen is a chimney on stilts—brick was expensive, so Myers bought only what was absolutely necessary. Clothes were handed down from oldest to youngest and when they became threadbare, they were recycled as rag rugs, called "clippy mats" in New England.

Visiting the house today is not so much like touring a museum as calling on friends. The tea is always on and cookies fresh from the wood stove are served by guides who know the region, lifestyle, and family. Times are better for fishing families today, but the museum helps remind us what we have, rather than what we don't have.

Visiting this tiny house is like calling on friends—cookies fresh from the wood stove and tea await.

Call (902) 889-2053
Open June 1–Oct 15,
Mon.–Sat. 9:30–5:30,
Sun. 1–5:30

Directions: On Highway 7, between Halifax and Sheet Harbour, Head for Jeddore Oyster Pond. The museum is at 58 Navy Pool Loop.

Sherbrooke Village

Sherbrooke Village is so pretty it would make set designers at Disney envious.

Originally settled by the French in 1655, in the 1800s the village was named to honour Lieutenant-Governor Sir John Sherbrooke. A once-prosperous community, Sherbrooke's economy was based on the traditional three Fs: farming, forestry, and fishery. It exported these products to Britain and the Caribbean. Adding to the community's prosperity was an 1861 gold rush.

Today Sherbrooke Village is a twenty-six building, two-mill complex owned by the Nova Scotia Museum. In the class of a living history museum —there are people in period costume throughout the community who explain life in 1860— Sherbrooke is different from the others. For one thing, every building in Sherbrooke is on its original foundation. Most historical villages are an amalgam of recycled buildings brought to one site.

The riverside setting is so calm and cozy, it's easy to understand the mythical attraction of the "good ol' days." In the centre of the village is a fenced paddock where horses frolic behind the blacksmith shop. Across the street from the smithy is the Sherbrooke Hotel, which is still open as a restaurant. Around the corner is the tiny post office and the print shop.

In the fully stocked apothecary shop women demonstrate pill making–a form of self-sufficiency now taken for granted. At the tailor shop women weren't allowed in the storefront–they were

Sherbrooke Village buildings, although reconstructed, sit on their original foundations.

Marine Drive

relegated to heating irons and sewing in the back room. The village jail was used until 1968. Men were imprisoned on the main level, and women were held upstairs. Interestingly, women were often jailed for their husband's debts. (In the last century men paid their debts quickly to get their wives out of the "hoosegow," when shame was still a deterrent to wrongdoing.)

The village's main street reveals an egalitarian community, where shops, services, and people of different backgrounds lived side by side. The doctor's house contains a surgery full of scary equipment (there are needles big enough to make a horse

Horses graze behind the blacksmith shop while work carries on inside as if it were 1860.

faint!). And from the outside the soaring Victorian merchant's house (Greenwood Cottage) is strikingly impressive.

The village is an interesting mix of past and present. While the Temperance Hall has been turned into an exhibition space, it is also home to the Sherbrooke Royal Canadian Legion, which out of deference to the building's history is "dry." The Masonic Hall is still used by the masons, St. James Presbyterian Church's congregation conducts services in the village, and the classically styled court house is still used for real trials.

Sherbrooke Village is a star in the provincial museum collection. There are wagon rides, street theatre, and items made on site are sold in the museum shop. (Note: For those with an allergy to bees, be careful. There are some hives and lots of wildflowers on site.) The only problem with visiting Sherbrooke is an invariable desire to move in.

"Old-fashioned" looking pottery pieces are made on site.

Sherbrooke Village "residents" bring the past to life.

Directions: Sherbrooke is on Highway 7, two and a half hours from Halifax or forty-five minutes from Antigonish.

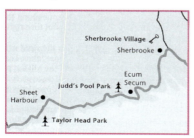

(902) 522-2400
1-888-743-7845
Open daily,
June 1–Oct 15
9:30–5:30

47c Canso Museum and Grassy Island National Historic Site

Canso is like many Nova Scotian communities, developed to tap into the forests and fishery. It also engaged in a little smuggling—resistance to taxes wasn't just the right of angry Bostonians.

The municipal museum, Whitman House, tells the local social history: the role Canso played in the Second World War, the shipping and fishery industries, and the community's involvement in transatlantic cable communication. In addition to the old mine detecting kit are ancient navigational items like an azimuth. Equally interesting is the fact that American patriot John Paul Jones attacked Canso in 1776. Jones sank one ship, destroyed two more, and took a third captive.

Grassy Island and Canso share a turbulent history that is chronicled at Grassy Island interpretation centre.

One of the interesting features of Whitman House is the widow's walk, a traditional rooftop feature which supposedly let wives watch for their husbands' return from sea. Whitman's walk is open to the public.

Down the road from the Whitman House is the Grassy Island National Historic Site. There's an interpretation centre and ferry service to the harbour island where the original European settlement was located.

Canso has a surprisingly violent history. The French came for the fishery, and were driven out by New Englanders. They were later attacked by the

French and Indians. Eventually, the British settled the island for its easy defence. The end came for both sides in 1744, when the French at Louisbourg got news of war with England before it reached the British in Annapolis Royal. The French attacked and destroyed Canso. This so alarmed the New Englanders they retaliated by attacking Louisbourg a year later.

No wonder Grassy Island was described as "full of fish and fighting men." Canso was such a prize because the fishery was rich—in the eighteenth century as much as 8 million fish were landed in a season.

Grassy Island used to be described as "full of fish and fighting men."

A less turbulent Grassy Island and Canso are ideal for hearty visitors seeking an historical adventure.

Directions: Whitman House is at 1297 Union Street and Grassy Island National Historic Site is located on the same street; the island is 1 km (0.6 mi.) off the coast of Canso.

Whitman House
(902) 366-2170
Open daily
May 15–Oct. 15, 9–6

Grassy Island
National Historic Site
(902) 366-2170
Open daily
June 1–Sept. 15, 10–6

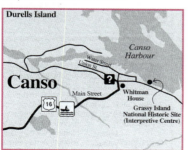

Marine Drive   61

The Canso area was considered a prize among warring nations for its rich fishery in the 1700s.

Halifax Metro Area

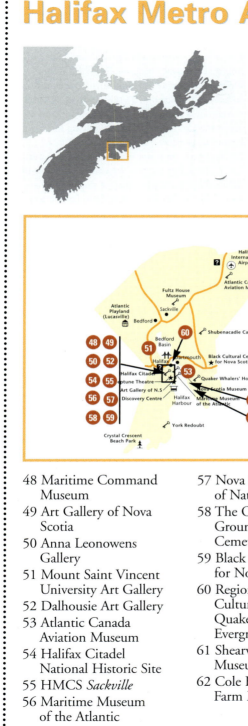

48 Maritime Command Museum
49 Art Gallery of Nova Scotia
50 Anna Leonowens Gallery
51 Mount Saint Vincent University Art Gallery
52 Dalhousie Art Gallery
53 Atlantic Canada Aviation Museum
54 Halifax Citadel National Historic Site
55 HMCS *Sackville*
56 Maritime Museum of the Atlantic
57 Nova Scotia Museum of Natural History
58 The Old Burying Ground (St. Paul's Cemetery)
59 Black Cultural Centre for Nova Scotia
60 Regional Museum of Cultural History, Quaker House and Evergreen House
61 Shearwater Aviation Museum
62 Cole Harbour Heritage Farm Museum

Maritime Command Museum

Within Maritime Command Museum, Admiralty House is the type of solid, grand, Georgian mansion that screams "Britannia Rules the Waves." Only an empire would build such an architectural treasure. Completed in 1818, the building served as the admiral's home until 1904. Now it is the Maritime Command Museum, tracing the navy's history in Halifax.

The museum is not what one may expect from a military collection. It is very human and personal. While there is a large display of ship's models—everything from a seventy-four gun French warship to the latest destroyers in the fleet—the museum has very few weapons on display. Instead, the focus is on naval life—much of it lived in peace.

The main level houses a large uniform collection, from the cocked hats and gold embroidered officer's waistcoats to seamen's skivvies. Upstairs the WRENS' (Women's Royal Naval Service) room is filled with examples of the first uniforms worn by WRENS.

The second floor focuses on the eighteenth and nineteenth century Royal Navy. It is a salty and stark story of Halifax press gangs where naval justice came with a "Kiss o' the Cat," and medical treatment wasn't much better. Early navy doctors are described as "misfits," who used saws and hot pitch to treat wounds.

In a way, this military museum seems a contradiction. It details the brutality of the old navy, celebrates the freedom won, yet does not boast. This museum is not about conquest or winning, it's about service. It is an intriguingly honest representation of naval life, from the serene third-floor remembrance window, the King's thanks to Silver Cross mothers, to music and artistic life, and a positively gory 1805 operating room guaranteed to thrill children.

Directions: Admiralty House is located at CFB Halifax on Gottingen Street, between North and Almon Streets. Don't use the main base gates. The museum has its own entrance; look for the huge white posts in the stone wall.

Admiralty House, a British admiral's home until 1904, now contains a broad collection that follows naval history in Halifax.

(902) 427-0550 ext. 8250
Open year-round
Mon.–Fri. 10–3:30
closed weekends

Art Gallery of Nova Scotia

The Art Gallery of Nova Scotia (AGNS) houses a four thousand work collection of historic, contemporary, Maritime and Canadian paintings, sculpture, and folk art, in an elegant and comfortable building.

Some describe folk art as naive. Others think it crude. Some have tried to categorize it as art which uses found materials, or adapts non-traditional art forms (woodworking, for example) with everyday materials (like house paint). Whatever the definition, folk art is fun. It's bright, light, amusing. Sometimes it looks as if it could only have been done by children. But it is this uninhibited wonder which gives many pieces their profundity. Folk art is also a type of political cartoon which relies less on a politician or authority figure to satirize than it does a cultural cliché or human trait.

The AGNS is home to a large collection of the folk art of Maud Lewis, Nova Scotia's Grandma Moses. In spite of her difficult life, Lewis' work is always cheerful, always positive.

The AGNS collection also includes works from Flemish religious paintings to woodblock prints and to artists such as Tom Forrestall, Alex Colville, Christopher Pratt, Ken Tolmie, Brother Thomas, A. J. Casson, Bruno Bobak, Lawren S. Harris, Guido Molinari, among others.

Folk art is just one exhibit gallery goers can see at the AGNS. The Education Gallery offers interactive exhibitions for kids.

The AGNS has galleries on three levels. On the lower level is the Education Gallery with interactive exhibitions geared to kids. There is also an art rental office and a gift shop. The AGNS is housed in the former Dominion Custom House at Cheapside—look for the figure of Britannia on the roof across from Province House.

With traffic sweeping by Hollis Street and the bustle of a modern city, the AGNS is an oasis in a sea of noise.

Directions: The AGNS is at 1741 Hollis Street, Halifax.

(902) 424-7542
Open year-round
Tues.–Fri. 10–5
Sat. and Sun. noon–5
Free admission on Tues.

Anna Leonowens Gallery

The Anna Leonowens Gallery is named for the woman who danced with the King of Siam in the Broadway musical, *The King and I*.

Leonowens, who returned to Halifax after her exotic appointment as a governess in the Siamese Court, was responsible for founding the Victoria School of Art and Design, now the Nova Scotia College of Art and Design. The Leonowens Gallery is located in the lower level of the art college in Historic Properties and features three street-level exhibition spaces. The gallery mandate is to exhibit work related to the activities at the college. Shows tend to favour the very edgy, avant-garde work created by the college's students, faculty, alumni and visiting artists. It's a very busy place, averaging 130 exhibitions a year.

Situated in the downtown core, the Leonowens Gallery, features shows by NSCAD students and faculty.

The Leonowens Gallery is a refreshing change from the highly representational art found in many East Coast collections and exhibit spaces. The gallery host lectures, video screenings and performances as well.

Directions: The gallery is located at 1891 Granville Street, as part of Granville Mall at Historic Properties, Halifax.

(902) 494-8223
Open year-round; closed the last two weeks of August; closed Sun. & Mon. Galleries are wheelchair accessible, but not the washrooms.

Mount Saint Vincent University Art Gallery

Mount Saint Vincent University (MSVU) is a Catholic-run institution which initially served an all-female population. The MSVU Art Gallery uses the continued women's focus as the artistic mandate. The gallery hosts changing exhibits of contemporary art and themes. Exhibitions range from textiles, pottery, and paintings by contemporary Nova Scotian artists, or themes related to the local community.

Directions: Mount Saint Vincent University Art Gallery is located in the Seton Academic Centre on campus, 166 Bedford Highway, Halifax.

Changing exhibits at the Mount Saint Vincent University Art Gallery reveal wide-ranging themes that focus on women's artistic work.

(902) 457-6160
Open year-round
Tues.–Fri. 11–5
Sat. & Sun. 1–5
closed Mon.

Dalhousie Art Gallery

Dalhousie Art Gallery focuses on contemporary and historical art in various media. Shows change every six weeks. A film program is held on Wednesdays.

Dalhousie Art Gallery exhibits change regularly so there's new work to see all the time.

Call (902) 494-2403
Open Tues.–Sun. 11–4;
closed Mondays; some variation in summer schedule. Call for details.

Directions: The gallery is located in the Rebecca Cohn Arts Centre (lower level), on the Dalhousie University campus, University Avenue in Halifax.

Atlantic Canada Aviation Museum

An exact replica of the Silver Dart stands above a Canadair CF-104 jet Starfighter, making a poignant statement by contrast. The *Silver Dart* is a poetic, frail-looking, rickety mesh of bamboo, canvas, wire, and hope. It's difficult to believe such things flew or that anyone would be brave enough to crawl on board. But this machine, designed by the Aerial Experiment Association of which Alexander Graham Bell was a member, did manage to make the first flight in the British Empire across a frozen Bras d'Or Lake in 1909, setting the Imperial record. The Starfighter illustrates the other extremes of aviation, the technical might and sophistication of Mach 2 speed.

A *Silver Dart* replica recalls aviation experiments conducted by Alexander Graham Bell and colleagues.

The aviation museum is deceptively large—there is a second gallery hidden by trees. The collection ranges from early aerial photographs circa 1883 to prisoner-of-war memorabilia of World War I and II to supersonic flight. And the names of aircraft mirror this devilish swagger and roaring recklessness: Harvard, Sabre, Canuck, Tracker, Starfighter, and Freedom Fighter.

The aviation collection goes well beyond military applications. There is a Canso Amphibian, a Jetstar, an Airliner, a glider, and a history of commercial aviation in Nova Scotia, and its role in agriculture (crop dusting).

(902) 873-3773
Open May 21–Oct. 15, daily 9–5

Those who are skittish fliers might not want to see the bikelike frame for the two-seat Aeronca C-3's. And to appreciate the "compactness" in which fighter pilots work, look into the Canadair T-33 Silver Star's cockpit.

The Atlantic Canada Aviation Museum—one of three in the province—is a great busman's holiday for pilots (past and present), and those interested in the technical and personal side of the province's aviation history.

Directions: The museum is located across Highway 102 from the Halifax International Airport. Take Exit 6 and follow the signs to the Airport Hotel and Visitor Information Centre.

Halifax Citadel National Historic Site

A window-rattling blast of a noon-day gun fired from the Halifax Citadel is a continual reminder of the military presence in the everyday life, and history, of this city by the sea.

An aerial view of Halifax Citadel shows off its strategic location in the capital.

The Army Museum is on site at the Citadel. It houses interesting army artifacts.

The present Citadel is the fourth fortification to don the hill in the centre of peninsular Halifax. When this fortress was built in 1855 it was the most technologically advanced military installation in the world. The Citadel was the centrepiece of a defence system that surrounded Halifax Harbour with forts, towers, and gun batteries. Although it is a tribute to imperial engineering, it was never challenged by an enemy.

The Citadel National Historic Site has three parts. First, is the fortress itself. Visitors can roam the walls (be careful of the 9 m/30 ft. drop), magazines, parade square, barracks, and watch the changing of the guard and firing of the cannon.

In one corner of the fortress, surrounded by its own solid stone wall, is the main powder magazine. Pushing a button inside this dark, barrel-filled building can unleash an abusive tirade from a mannequin guarding the magazine. This invective cleverly explains the extensive precautions once taken to prevent an explosion.

Discover Nova Scotia Museums and Art Galleries

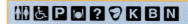

The second part of the Citadel is a small city museum built into the fortress walls. It covers the history of Halifax from its founding in 1749 to the present.

The third element is the Army Museum in the building which dominates the parade square. This is a volunteer-run museum, separate from the Citadel proper. The Army Museum deals solely with the army: the uniforms, weapons, kit, campaigns, experiences and sacrifices, from colonial militia to imperial force to commonwealth partner.

One of the more poignant displays includes plaques for three members of one family killed in World War I, accompanied by the Silver Cross Mother Pins. The Army Museum displays the implements of war and chronicles their use, but does not glorify might and conflict. It is a respectful remembrance of the harsh toll inflicted on people.

Life in the 1800s is portrayed in living colour.

The 78th Highlanders re-enact a rifle exercise on parade square of Citadel Hill.

The Citadel is Canada's most visited national historic site. And it's probably the only site in Canada with moat parking.

Directions: The Citadel is located in the centre of Halifax. By car, approach from Sackville Street or walk up the steps from Brunswick Street past the Town Clock (across from the Metro Centre).

(902) 426-5080
Open
May 15–June 14
& Sept. 1–Oct.15
8:45–5
June 15–Aug. 31
8:45–6

HMCS *Sackville*

While not technically part of the Maritime Museum of the Atlantic, HMCS *Sackville* continues the story begun there. HMCS *Sackville* is a corvette, a 62.5 m (205 ft.) long, "little" ship designed for coastal patrol. However, they were pressed into service accompanying World War II convoys from Halifax to Britain, and were a major player in the Battle of the Atlantic.

During World War II, corvettes like the HMCS *Sackville* bobbed along like corks on the ocean chasing submarines.

The *Sackville* is a hands-on study into the claustrophobic living conditions and life aboard a Corvette. Below decks, crewmen were practically stacked on top of each other. On such a small ship every inch of space is maximized. The sick bay is little more than a closet with shelves. Cramped and cold, corvettes bobbed like corks in water, and were the wettest, most uncomfortable ships in the naval arsenal.

On the outdoor bridge is a set of funnel-shaped brass-topped tubes through which the captain shouted orders. Clustered like a garden of spitoons, each tube is connected to a different section of the ship.

Typically, battleships which make it to museum status are wooden sailing vessels that embrace the romantic and heroic past of a Nelson at Trafalgar. HMCS *Sackville* is a rarity because is it the last surviving corvette, and one of the few warships of the modern era available for viewing. (Note: Be careful on the ship's steps, they're more like ladders. It is best to go up forward and down backwards.)

HMCS *Sackville* should be seen, not just because it's Canada's Naval Memorial, but to understand the sacrifice of men at war. There was no privacy, no comfort, and limited armaments. All this ship had was speed, manoeuvrability, and crews dedicated to God, King and Country.

Directions: HMCS *Sackville* is moored at Sackville Landing wharf, behind the Maritime Museum of the Atlantic on Lower Water Street, Halifax.

Ship: (902) 429-2132,
Office: (902) 427-0550, ext. 2837
Open Mid–June to Sept. 30,
Mon.–Sat. 10–5, Sun. 1–5

Maritime Museum of the Atlantic

She's tall and pale with a bright red sash. She's the figurehead of the Imaum, a seventy-two gun warship launched from Bombay in 1826. Once a world traveller, she now greets visitors to the Maritime Museum of the Atlantic.

The Maritime Museum details the importance of the sea to Halifax, to Nova Scotia and to Canada. It tracks the grandeur and romance of the golden age of travel, of wooden ships and iron men, of the once mighty Canadian Navy (it grew from 13 ships in 1939 to 450 combat ships by 1945), of Haligonians like Sir Samuel Cunard, and disasters like the Halifax Explosion.

The front of the museum holds the chandlery, a creaky, musty rope-smelling store which "provisions" ships. The museum's main gallery contains a diverse collection of wooden boats. The self-baling Sable Island lifeboat is eerily described as "virtually unsinkable" (all the more spine-chilling since the museum has an HMS *Titanic* display—complete with one of those oft-mentioned deck chairs). Further on is the Goose Boat. Built in 1900 by a Presbyterian minister to sneak up on game birds resting in ice fields, the front of the Goose Boat looks like an old submarine, while the rear is like a large, sling-back shoe.

Across the gallery sits the white, gold, and green Royal Barge. Commissioned by the Lords of the Admiralty to mark Queen Victoria's 1877 Jubilee, the barge was a gift from Queen Elizabeth to the museum. With an ornately carved royal cipher, bronzed dolphin oar locks, and serpent-shaped rudder, the barge could belong to no one but an empress—it makes an impression.

Don't expect to breeze through this museum. It is a foundation piece to understanding Nova Scotia's social, economic and military structure.

Directions: The museum is at 1675 Lower Water Street, Halifax.

Maritime Museum of the Atlantic is a compelling look at the sea's influence.

(902) 424-7490
Open year-round
June 1–Oct.15
Mon., Wed. & Sat. 9:30–5:30;
Tues. 9:30–8; Sun. 1–5:30

Nova Scotia Museum of Natural History

"Where are the bees?" is the most asked question at the Nova Scotia Museum of Natural History. The popular bee display is a cross-section of a live hive connected to the outside world. Visitors get to see the bees at work and how "guard bees" protect the colony entrance.

Discover the province's natural wonders at the Nova Scotia Museum.

As the name suggests, the museum explores the natural history of Nova Scotia through the creation of the present land mass and the prehistoric creatures that roamed Nova Scotia.

One of the museum's larger exhibits is dedicated to Nova Scotia's moving island—Sable Island. Christened the Graveyard of the Atlantic, it is a mysterious, fragile ecosystem—not much more than a moving sand bar held together by marsh grass—notorious for shipwrecks and famous for wild horses.

However, the collection is not just rocks, fossils, and taxidermy. There is a strong human element.

Live creatures add to the drama of museum displays.

For instance, the museum examines the province's earliest known residents who lived around Debert eleven thousand years ago, and the pre-deportation life of the Acadians. The collections do not gloss over history, as evidenced by the unsavoury habits of the troops stationed in Fort Lawrence: from what archaeologists have uncovered, garrison life seemed limited to drinking, smoking, and shooting pigs—not much of a legacy.

There is a stunning display of Mi'kmaq costumes and porcupine quillwork. One outfit, circa 1841, displays rare examples of appliqué, beadwork, and double-stitched curve sewing.

The museum's quillwork collection of decorative boxes, chairs, and tables from 1700 to 1940 is one of the world's finest. It follows the development of this art form from natural dyes to commercial colourings introduced by European settlers.

And don't miss the Lorenzen Mushroom display. These two hundred mushrooms are so finely crafted, so exquisitely detailed, it's impossible to believe they're man-made.

Rocks, minerals, animals, puffins, whale

skeletons, mastodon bones and inventive educational programs for children: the Museum of Natural History is neither static nor stuffy; it's just a great place to visit.

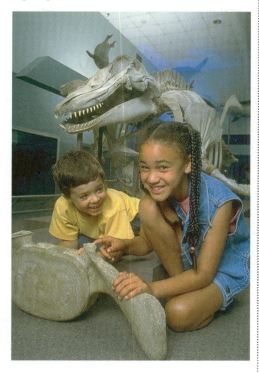

Children especially enjoy the models of Canada's oldest dinosaurs.

(902) 424-7353
Open Year-round
June 1–Oct. 15
Mon.-Sat. 9:30–5:30
Wed. 9:30–8
Sun. 1–5:30
Oct. 16–May 31
Tues.–Sat. 9:30–5
Wed. 9:30–8
Admission charged
June 1–Oct. 15

Directions: The museum entrance is at 1747 Summer Street (near the Public Gardens) in Halifax.

Halifax Metro Area

The Old Burying Ground (St. Paul's Cemetery)

Halifax's Old Burying Ground or St. Paul's Cemetery—it's the one with the arch and lion across from Government House—is the first in Canada to be designated a national historic site as one of the most important cemeteries in Canada.

Even though twelve thousand people are buried here, the Old Burying Ground should be regarded as an outdoor museum, a walk through history, and an open air art gallery. It's a sculpture garden that reveals the history of the colony, of early commerce (gravestones were imported from Massachusetts until the American Revolution created our own monument industry), views on death, and the evolution of funereal art. Now funeral art may sound grim, but it's bizarrely beautiful, and that's why this cemetery is so important.

The twelve hundred gravestones in provide an important look at rare examples of pre-Victorian grave art. Older stones portray death in a stylized form, employing winged skulls (called "death heads") and angels.

The cemetery was granted by the Crown to St. Paul's Church in 1793 and used until 1830. It reveals a great deal about attitudes and funereal art.

By the early 1800s, however, monument imagery changed from representations of death to bereavement. The mourner's grief was depicted by funeral urns, extinguished lamps of life, and weeping willows.

What makes this cemetery interesting is its personality. These stones tell stories of infants taken by disease, women who died in childbirth, epidemics, loved ones lost at sea, generous acts, and a few recriminations. One stone near the Spring Garden Road Courthouse is less a memorial than a stinging indictment of the deceased's murderer, who is not only named, but called names.

Call for information (902) 426-5080. Open June–Sept.

Strange as it may seem, the Old Burying Ground offers a compelling glimpse into social, cultural, and historical attitudes. Information and maps are available year-round at St. Paul's Church at the Grand Parade on Barrington Street.

Directions: The cemetery is located on Barrington Street, opposite Government House.

The Black Cultural Centre for Nova Scotia

The first black to arrive in what is now Nova Scotia came with the first French settlers in 1606. Sadly, albeit typically, he was not a free man.

While much of the history of the province leads one to believe this was a land inhabited by whites and Mi'kmaq, black Nova Scotians have been here from the start of European settlement. Their efforts, struggles, and accomplishments are preserved in the Black Cultural Centre for Nova Scotia through ongoing programming, monthly events, and special celebrations. The centre is also the main repository of the history of Blacks.

Black history and culture are depicted in thematic displays.

One wall of the centre's main room traces the black migration to and from Nova Scotia. Few people realize there were black United Empire Loyalists (UELs). Beginning in 1783, thirty-five hundred black UELs came to Nova Scotia. Having fought for the British Crown in the American Revolution, they were rewarded with their freedom. However, that freedom was rather dubious, since they were consistently mistreated and cheated out of promised land grants.

The centre maintains a room dedicated to choral history, as well as an exhibit on two of the province's most famous citizens: opera singer Portia White and war hero William Hall. White's career took her around the world. It was because of her that the Nova Scotia Talent Trust, which still exists, was created to help deserving artists. Hall received the Victoria Cross, the Empire's highest award for valour, for his participation in the Indian Mutiny.

Visitors will learn that many Black communities exist in Nova Scotia, that there was a special World War I Black Battalion, and that segregation existed in Nova Scotia well into the 1950s. Miles travelled and miles to go.

(902) 434-6223 or
1-800-465-0767
Open year-round,
Mon.–Fri. 9–5,
June–Sept.
Sat. 10–4

Directions: Follow Route 7 in Dartmouth to 1149 Main Street (near the Preston/Cherry Brook area).

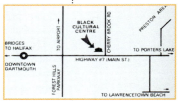

Halifax Metro Area

Regional Museum of Cultural History, Quaker House and Evergreen House

The Mi'kmaq were the first people to live in what is now Dartmouth. They came every spring from inland encampments to hunt, fish, gather berries, and make pottery. In 1750 the English settled Dartmouth as a type of colonial suburb, integrating the settlement into the harbour's defence system. The Regional Museum of Cultural History explores the natural, historical, and cultural heritage of the community.

Housed in a former city hall, the museum's main floor is used for changing exhibitions. The museum is also a centre for art shows, author's readings, and a venue for the Eastern Front Theatre. So, walking in the door can be a constant surprise.

Artifact collections at the Regional Museum focus on social history with an emphasis on Dartmouth and surrounding area.

Upstairs, the main gallery displays a collection ranging from Nova Scotia's first mega-project: the 80 km (50 mi.) long Shubenacadie Canal, built to speed troop movement between the Bay of Fundy and Atlantic shores; to tributes to famous Dartmouthians like Joseph Howe and William Rowe. Rowe is the ship's architect responsible for the *Bluenose*. Howe was the crusading newspaper publisher who won freedom of the press for all the British Empire in 1835.

Evergreen House, built in 1867, contains fine pieces from the Regional Museum's collection of Victorian furniture.

One of the museum's more thought-provoking displays deals with the Halifax Explosion. Because of its name—the Halifax Explosion—many people forget Dartmouth was also devastated.

The Regional Museum oversees the Quaker House built in 1786 and the newer (1867) Evergreen House. The houses show how society grew and what their owners believed. The Quaker House is about simplicity and function (note the massive fireplaces). Evergreen House is a Victorian celebration of wealth and position. Originally built for a judge, it was later owned by folklorist and author Helen Creighton.

The Regional Museum complex is a worthwhile drive across the harbour.

(902) 464-2300 Open year-round daily 10–4; Quaker House (902) 464-2253 & Evergreen House (902) 466-2301 are open only in summer or by appointment.

Quaker House, built by Nantucket Quaker whalers, is the oldest home in Dartmouth.

Directions: The Regional Museum Complex is at 100 Wyse Road by the Dartmouth Commons. Turn right off the MacDonald Bridge. Quaker House is at 57-59 Octerloney Street; Evergreen House is at 26 Newcastle Street, Dartmouth.

Shearwater Aviation Museum

If you thought two-seater, open-cockpit biplanes died out with the Red Baron, think again. They were still in use during the Second World War. The gem of the Shearwater Aviation Museum collection is just such an artifact: a 1932 Fairey Swordfish biplane—one of only four in the world in airworthy condition.

The Shearwater Aviation Museum collection contains a variety of artifacts and aircraft spanning the base's history from 1918 to the present.

Housed in a hangar on the edge of CFB Shearwater, the biplane looks suspiciously familiar to anyone who has owned a British sports car: same seats, same dash. The rear-mounted machine gun seems frighteningly inadequate. It was this type of fragile-looking plane which landed a torpedo on the infamous German battleship *Bismarck*, disabling it long enough for the navy to come and "sink the Bismarck."

The Shearwater Aviation Museum tells the history of the air force in Nova Scotia from 1918 to the present. Surprisingly, Shearwater was originally formed during World War I as United States Naval Air Station Halifax, and placed under the command of Lieutenant R. E. Byrd, later Admiral Byrd, the polar explorer. The first American squadron flew patrols over a 129 km (80 mi.) zone from Liverpool to Liscomb Mills because all Canadian forces were committed to the European theatre.

Since CFB Shearwater is "the Wing of the

Fleet," it has displays and a large-scale model of Canada's last aircraft carrier, HMCS *Bonaventure*, along with the original seats from the ship's briefing room. To the left of the model is a gyro-mounted mirror used on the *Bonaventure* to guide pilots onto the deck. By lining up an amber dot— "the meat ball"—in the centre of the mirror, the pilot could pick up an "arrestor wire," which would

Pictured here flying over Halifax in 1994, the Fairey Swordfish at Shearwater is one of only four airworthy examples worldwide.

safely stop his plane on the carrier deck and not in the drink.

Upstairs in the museum is a vivid and interesting gallery of military aviation art.

One of the amusing and surprising artifacts on display is a pigeon basket. During the Second World War, amid all the new technology developed to fight a fully mechanized war, pilots observed radio silence by releasing homing pigeons from their aircraft in order to send a message. This dusty wicker basket and accompanying explanation, set among radar and sonar displays, shows the eccentricity of modern warfare. War really is won on a wing and a prayer.

Directions: Located just outside the base gate at 12 Wing, Shearwater, Dartmouth. Follow Pleasant Street (Highway 322), past the oil refinery, toward Fisherman's Cove to 13 Bonaventure Avenue heading up to the Shearwater Airport.

(902) 460-1083
Open April 1–Nov. 30
other times by appointment
July & Aug.
Tues.–Fri. 10–5,
Sat. & Sun. noon–4
Other months
Tues., Wed., & Thurs. 10–5, Sat. noon–4

Cole Harbour Heritage Farm

Surrounded by urban sprawl, the Cole Harbour Heritage Farm Museum is a serene 1 ha (2.5 acre) site just two blocks from the suburbs. The farm museum is not glamourous but it offers a glimpse into an endangered way of life.

This is a great place for families to visit. It has all the barnyard sounds and smells. Cocks crow, cows moo, horses whinny, pigs grunt and skittish chickens scratch at the ground.

The Cole Harbour Heritage Farm is significant because, for centuries, this was Halifax's garden. Farmers supplied Halifax markets since Cole Harbour's salt-marsh and well-drained lands could support agriculture, while much of the land near the capital was too rocky to farm.

The Giles House (top, right) and a cultivator (bottom) are good examples of eighteenth-century farm life preserved here.

The museum includes a blacksmith's shop, old farm implements, wagons, and fishery displays. Cole Harbour is rich in rivers, brooks and harbours from which early settlers caught eels, salmon, trout, gaspereau, lobster, and clams to sell to Haligonians.

The Giles House, an eighteenth-century farmhouse, shows how a farm family lived in 1786. Watch your head, the ceilings are low. The farm operates a charming country-style tea room serving fresh pies.

There is even a nature trail on site with a forest, a meadow, and a small lake.

(902) 462-0154
Open mid-May–Oct. 15;
other times by appointment;
Mon.–Sat. 10–4
Sun. & holidays 12–4

Directions: Follow Cole Harbour Road (Route 207) to Otago Drive. From Dartmouth, turn left at the traffic lights opposite the mall. Proceed to 471 Poplar Drive in Cole Harbour.

Lighthouse Route

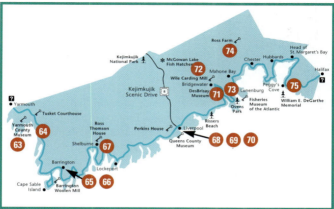

63 Wedgeport Sport Tuna Fishing Museum
64 Argyle Township Courthouse and Gaol
65 The Old Meeting House Museum (Barrington)
66 Barrington Woolen Mill
67 Ross-Thomson House and Store Museum, Shelburne County Museum, and J.C. Williams Dory Shop
68 Perkins House Museum Queens County Museum
69 Sherman Hines Museum of Photography and Art Galleries
70 Hank Snow Country Music Centre
71 DesBrisay Museum
72 Wile Carding Mill Museum
73 Fisheries Museum of the Atlantic & Lunenburg Art Gallery
74 Ross Farm Museum
75 William E. deGarthe Gallery

63 Wedgeport Sport Tuna Fishing

Tiny Wedgeport (population 1,698) on the southern tip of Nova Scotia is a place people typically drive by. But for those who were fishermen anytime between 1935 and 1970, Wedgeport was an alluring spot.

In its glory days Wedgeport was the sport tuna fishing capital of the world. The rich and famous flocked here the way they do now in Vail and Aspen. It's amazing to note who has been here: Kate Smith, Amelia Earhart, Gene Tunney, Jean Beliveau, Franklin D. Roosevelt, Zane Grey, Robert Maytag, Ernest Hemingway.

For many years, bluefin tuna were considered nothing but a nuisance because they wrecked fishing nets. Along the way, someone discovered the taste and the sport these fish could provide a determined, and fit, angler. Tuna are not tiny fish. They are huge, as evidenced by the stuffed tuna on display at the Wedgeport Sport Tuna Fishing Museum. Tuna are so large, fishermen would harpoon them!

Tuna fishing in Wedgeport provides industry and sport for locals and famous visitors to the area.

This is a new museum and displays are still developing, but the core artifacts do tell a good story. The tuna boat with rod and reel shows how fishers battled the big fish. There are also videos, a fish tank, and displays devoted to the history of the Acadians and of Wedgeport. There is also a nature trail on site to explore.

The museum is connected to the tuna guide association club house, so it's possible to chat with men who know the fishery intimately. Periodically the museum organizes boat tours (which must be arranged in advance) of the Tusket Islands.

(902) 663-4345
Open mid-June–mid-Sept.
daily 9–6

Directions: The museum is on Route 334, 15 km (9 mi.) from Yarmouth. Follow the signs.

Argyle Township Courthouse and Gaol

This is the oldest courthouse and jail in Canada. It dates from 1805 and was built with the idea of inflicting punishment. There was no thought given to the rehabilitation of criminals. Here criminals sat in dark cells all day (candles were a fire hazard) presumably contemplating their misdeeds. The only time prisoners left their cells was to use the toilet which amounted to a chamber pot in a hall closet. The "washroom" is so small the door couldn't be shut when occupied.

A taste of nineteenth-century justice is offered at the Argyle Township Courthouse and Gaol.

The gaol (English spelling) is like a large walk-in vault, only slightly better than a medieval dungeon. It is entered through a heavy iron door into a narrow, whitewashed hallway lined by grim little windowless cells. If a prisoner was lucky he had a cell with inch-thick iron bar doors, which allowed light to filter in. A double cell was used for debtors. Single cells have barely enough room for a cot. Solitary confinement was spent in a single cell with steel-plated walls.

Upstairs is the equally stern courtroom. The court's original furniture includes the clerks' table, in front of the judge's podium, with a grated shelf. This grate allowed the court minutes, which were written with by a quill dipped in ink, to dry without smudging.

The Argyle Township Courthouse and Gaol, a municipal museum site, offer a grim glimpse into the quick, harsh reality of the colonial legal system which was a black-and-white process. Guided tours are given. The Argyle Township Courthouse Archives are also here. The Courthouse and Gaol is well worth a visit.

Directions: From Highway 103, take Exit 33 and proceed along highway 3 to the courthouse at 8163 in Tusket.

(902) 648-2493
Open May to Oct.
daily in July & Aug.
9–5
other months
Mon.–Fri. 9–5.
Archives are open year-round
Mon.–Fri. 9–5

Lighthouse Route

65   The Old Meeting House (Barrington)

Separation of church and state was a concept lost on the Quaker and Congregationalists who settled Barrington. Believing church and state influence each other, in a marriage of thrift and principle they constructed one building to serve both purposes.

The Old Meeting House, built in 1761 in Barrington, is the only such structure left in the province. It is reminiscent of New England meeting houses and was used for religious services, town meetings and elections. The first floor has seating arranged in boxed pews. A balcony, added later, was for the lower class, non-land-owning members of the community. Quakers and Congregationalists may not have wanted a separation of church and state, but it appears they didn't relish mingling with their "social inferiors."

The people who came to Barrington were well-educated "friendly Protestants," encouraged to populate Nova Scotia after the Deportation of the Acadians. The idea was that Protestants would be more friendly to the British.

Inside, the building shows the shipbuilding background of the workmen who constructed it. Light floods the interior through 352 panes of glass. And the 51 cm (20 inch) wide floor boards show the virginal state of the colony's ancient forests. Perhaps the most interesting decorative feature is the upstairs colouring: the builders used a blueberry stain.

The Meeting House is an interesting study of conflicting beliefs: equality before God, but not for the neighbours. There is a type of parsimony associated with this austere building that makes it a thought-provoking stop. A graveyard next door is the resting place of early townspeople.

Directions: Follow Highway 3 to number 2408 in Barrington.

Boxed pews inside give a vivid impression of the Old Meeting House's original character.

(902) 637-2185
Open June 1–Sept. 30
Mon.–Sat. 9:30–5:30
Sun. 1–5:30

Barrington Woolen Mill

In the days before synthetics, people who worked outdoors—farmers, fishermen and loggers—needed warm, weatherproof clothing. In the nineteenth century that meant wool. As a result, many Nova Scotian families kept sheep for the wool and mutton.

Cleaning, carding, spinning, and weaving wool into cloth is labour-intensive work when done at home. So, when technology came to the community in the form of the Barrington Woolen Mill in 1882, some burden was lifted from the shoulders of local women.

The mill museum is exactly as it was in 1882. There have been no major changes in equipment or power source. This dark, well-worn building was so cold in winter that employees warmed themselves by standing on hot iron plates that were used to give a smooth finish to cloth. When the building was in full operation the air would be thick with fluff and dust. The noise from the leather belts flapping around the machinery, the clattering knitting machines, the woof of the looms, and roar of the water wheel were almost deafening. Quite a contradiction to the village's calm.

The Barrington Mill used an old-fashioned process to produce a quality product with a good reputation. However, in 1962 it was finally forced to close by competition from catalogue shopping, a change to wider cloth bolts, and cheap synthetic materials.

In its day, the Barrington Woolen Mill was a model of technological advancement. It was a hub of commercial activity and the hope for economic prosperity. Today, it helps explain the hard work that went into procuring the basic goods for day-to-day living. It provokes appreciation for the modern convenience to running into a shop to buy what we want, when we want it.

Directions: The museum is located in the centre of Barrington, by the bridge.

The mill thrived during war—armies needed uniforms and blankets—and supplied fishermen's warm woolen mitts.

(902) 637-2185
Open June 1–
Sept. 30
Mon.–Sat. 9:30–5:30
Sun. 1–5:30

67 Ross-Thomson House and Store Museum, Shelburne County Museum, and J. C. Williams Dory Shop

Ross-Thomson House reflects Loyalist lifestyle after the American Revolution.

The store and chandlery are authentically stocked.

Shelburne's waterfront remains virtually untouched since the town was founded by United Empire Loyalists in 1783. The only new structures—stocks, Guild Hall and Charburton Rooming House—were built as sets for the movie *A—The Scarlet Letter*. Everything else, is authentic.

Traffic is restricted in this enclave so it's a pleasant stroll among the restaurants, gift shop, art centre, and three museums: Ross-Thomson House and Store Museum, Shelburne County Museum, and J. C. Williams Dory Shop.

Among the ten thousand Loyalists who fled America after the revolution were George and Robert Ross. In 1785 the brothers built the Ross-Thomson House & Store. Now part of the Nova Scotia Museum family, the Ross-Thomson building contains a store, a militia display, and home. The house contents are all original: Chippendale chairs, pewter, incense burners (circa 1120 A. D.), to a Dickensian clerk's desk.

The Ross-Thomson House is approached through the small, fragrant, fenced garden of old style plants like Royal George Lustripe, Loyalist Rose, white strawberry, and Mandrake Apple.

Down the garden path is the treasure-box-like Shelburne County Museum. The main floor gallery is used for changing exhibits. A second room contains the oldest fire engine in Canada, if not all of North America. The 1740 English-made oak pumper resembles a child's wagon. It is small enough to be pulled inside a burning building and was used for 151 years before it was retired!

The museum's most eye-opening display deals with the one thousand Black United Empire Loyalists, who came to the area in 1783.

The third facility to see among Shelburne's museums is the waterside J. C. Williams Dory Shop. From 1880 until 1971, this shop launched more than ten thousand dories—all built using only hand tools.

Discover Nova Scotia Museums and Art Galleries

Shelburne has the third largest natural harbour in the world—after Halifax and Sydney, Australia—so shipbuilding, shipping, and fishing have always been economic staples. Dories were an important part of the fishery.

Dories may look like a glorified rowboat but, in fact, they are made with a very sophisticated design to survive the hostile Atlantic. They have numerous inventions to protect the fisherman and make his work safer.

For all their common characteristics, there are two specific types of dory: the Lunenburg and Shelburne dories. A Lunenburg dory uses a bent tree branch or root for its rib. The Shelburne dory uses a specially developed metal clip, which locks several pieces of wood together as one rib. This clip innovation allowed Shelburne makers to build dories more quickly than Lunenburgers.

Full-sized dories can be ordered from the men working upstairs in the museum—the ultimate souvenir.

Shelburne County Museum has displays on various aspects of local history.

J. C. Williams Dory Shop (below) still builds full-size dories.

Ross-Thomson House
(902) 875-3141
Open June 1–Oct.15
9:30–5:30
Shelburne County Museum
(902) 875-3219
Open year-round daily May 15–Oct.15
9:30–5:30
winter Tues.–Fri. 2–5
Sat. 9:30–12 & 2–5
Dory Shop
(902)875-3219
Open June 1–Sept. 30
9:30–5:30

Directions: Parking areas and restaurants are close to all three museums, and a tourism information centre is at the end of Dock Street. Picnic tables are located by the gallows. There is a Shelburne museum pass that saves money on admission prices. The Ross-Thomson House and Store Museum is at 9 Charlotte Street. The Shelburne County Museum is located on Maiden Lane.

Lighthouse Route

Perkins House Museum
Queens County Museum

Perkins House is the oldest house in the Nova Scotia Museum collection.

The history of Queens County is preserved in exhibits of artifacts from everyday life.

Simeon Perkins, whose diary provides a detailed record of life in Queens County from 1766 to 1812, was one of the prominent Planters who was recruited from New England to occupy the lands vacated by the deported Acadians. Perkins was an officer in the militia, a member of the legislature, a justice of the peace, a probate judge, and he was involved in privateering.

Perkins' 1766 Liverpool home, where he and his wife raised eight children, is the oldest site in the Nova Scotia Museum family. Like many older homes, the rooms are painted in glorious colours—deep green in the counting room, brown in the kitchen, red in the birthing/storage room. The furniture collection contains a 1779 Bible in its box, a portrait of Perkins, and a nanny's bench.

Although Queens County is famous for its forestry and fishery industries, privateering nd rum running played a part in its colorful history. The town of Liverpool became known as a centre for privateers, piracy licensed by the Crown, during the American/England wars.

All this history is crammed into the municipally operated Queens County Museum next door to Perkins House. The museum also contains the recreated study of Thomas H. Raddall, Nova Scotia's most famous author.

A small display of medical instruments from 1788 makes one appreciate the advances in modern medicine.

Directions: Perkins House is at 105 Main Street in Liverpool. Follow the key signs. The Queens County Museum in Liverpool is at 109 Main Street, next to Perkins House. The two sites share a parking lot.

Perkins House
(902) 354-4058
Open June 1–Oct.15.
Mon.–Sat. 9:30–5:30,
Sun. 1–5:30
Queens County Museum
(902) 354-4058
Open year-round
June–Oct.15
Mon.–Sat. 9:30–5:30
Sun. 1–5:30
Oct. 16–May 31
Mon.–Sat. 9–5

Sherman Hines Museum of Photography and Art Galleries

The Sherman Hines Museum of Photography and Art Galleries is a reminder that in the right hands, a camera can be every bit as effective and inspiring as a painter's brush or sculptor's chisel.

This museum is internationally renowned photographer/author Sherman Hines' homage to his art. Beginner and professional photographers alike will find the Sherman Hines Museum of Photography and Art Galleries holds something for everyone.

The facility takes visitors from high art to holiday snaps. There are wonderful old photos of favoured uncles, Imperial gatherings, and stuffy Victorians looking as important as they fancied they were. There are black-and-white landscape photographs that are so gentle they don't look real.

Naturally, the museum has an extensive camera collection. On the main level is the Camera Obscura. This is a darkened room which uses a pin-hole to project street scenes on a wall.

Other photographic devices include clunky antique boxes so heavy it would take two strong men to lift one, to fragile nineteenth-century lantern slides—small pictures hand-painted on glass which were passed through a lantern. The museum takes visitors from the days of dark cloth draped over a photographer's head as he holds a powder flash, to a holographic display.

Hines is democratic in assigning space. This building is not simply filled with his work. There are rare examples of W. R. MacAskill hand-tinted photographs, natural history displays, and changing shows by contemporary painters and photographers. The Sherman Hines Museum of Photography is so genuinely interesting, one wonders why it wasn't opened earlier. It is unique east of Montreal.

Directions: The museum and art gallery are located in the Old Town Hall, 219 Main Street in Liverpool.

The evolution of photography is presented in collections of equipment and the art itself at the Sherman Hines Museum.

(902) 354-2667
Open May 1–Dec. 23
Mon.–Sat. 10–5:30
& Sundays 12–5 in June, July & Aug.

70 Hank Snow Country Music Centre

What Queens County man recorded 100 albums, sold over 70 million records and had 60 Top Ten Hits? Hank Snow. And that's why his name is on the Hank Snow Country Music Centre in Liverpool's former railway station.

This stop is a must for country music lovers.

Before he established his place in country music with hits like "I'm Movin' On," "I've Been Everywhere," and "The Golden Rocket," Snow occasionally slept on the train station platform, which makes this all the more appropriate for a museum named in his honour.

But the centre is not an exclusive homage to him. It is dedicated to and features a variety of Canadian country music stars: Carole Baker, Tex Cochrane, Don Messer, Patsy Montana, Noel Landry, and Lucille Starr, among others.

The centre is also home to the new Nova Scotia Country Music Hall of Fame (it's surprising how many country stars come from Nova Scotia), a music archive, a library, and a gift shop. As well, the centre hosts music-based events.

This fun collection ranges from Snow's 1947 Cadillac, to uninhibited stage costumes favoured by country music stars, to an opportunity to set foot on the Grand Old Opry's stage—a round wood floor inset and backdrop came from the Opry.

One of the newest facilities in Nova Scotia—opened in 1996—The Hank Snow Country Music Centre will thrill country music fans and is worth a visit by anyone interested in music and/or a music career. Stars have to come from somewhere, and quite a few, we learn, come from Nova Scotia.

Call (902) 354-4675
Open May 1 to Thanksgiving other times by appointment.
July 1–Aug. 31
Mon.–Sat. 9–6
Sun. 12–6
other months
Mon.–Sat. 10–6
Sun. 12–6

Directions: From Route 8, take Exit 19 from Highway 103. The centre is about a minute's drive from the exit. The Hank Snow Centre is off Bristol Avenue in Liverpool.

DesBrisay Museum

While the Fisheries Museum focuses on the ocean-related economy, the DesBrisay Museum displays what happened ashore.

Lunenburg is a centre for decorative arts—folk artists are often off-season farmers and fishers—so there is a large collection devoted to folk art. Its fun, poignant, and sometimes mischievous form of expression employs the natural materials found

around the artists' homes—like left-over paint, an intriguing tree root, or a broken appliance.

The versatility and utility of the docile oxen that served Lunenburgers as a beast of burden and means of transportation is celebrated in an award-winning exhibit the DesBrisay developed on oxen.

The DesBrisay's prize possession is a multi-coloured quill-covered cradle. The quillwork was done by Christianna Morris, a Mi'kmaq artist whose work was chosen as a gift to the Prince of Wales.

The collection also includes ship models, furniture, Alice Hagen ceramics, and the famous Biscuit quilt (each patch has puffs of cotton that give a three-dimensional effect). The South Shore of Nova Scotia has long been famous for its fabrics: hooked rugs, sweaters, mitts, socks, and quilts.

Directions: Take Exit 13 from Highway 103 and follow the signs to 130 Jubilee Street in Bridgewater. Or, drive along King Street, toward LaHave, and turn south onto Jubilee Street.

The DesBrisay Museum collection includes intriguing works by local folk artists.

(902) 543-4033
Open year-round
seasonal hours

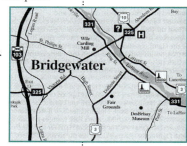

72 Wile Carding Mill Museum

Walking into the Wile Carding Mill in Bridgewater is like taking a time machine to the start of the Industrial Revolution. Inside is a large whitewashed main room. The ceiling is low. Through the open door a breeze blows scraps of wool across the worn, dark floorboards. Bags of wool slump against walls and machinery.

In the centre of the floor the massive machinery takes pride of place. The one creature comfort is the closet-sized, well-worn wooden toilet shoved into a far corner. Downstairs is the still-functional overshot water wheel.

Everything about this mill reeks of the grim austerity of Victorian factories. Owners lived comfortable lives surrounded by exotic and strange Victorian bric-a-brac, but workplaces were mercilessly functional. The Wile Mill furnishings consist of a stand-up desk, small wood stove, and a chair. To really understand the working conditions at the Wile Carding Mill, view the video at the DesBrisay Museum of a former worker telling her story.

When the Wile Carding Mill opened in 1860, it operated with three women working a seventy-two-hour week. They were paid two dollars a week.

With many farmers and fishermen living a subsistence life, the more a family produced at home, the better off they were financially. As a result everyone kept a few sheep. Carding mills could clean, pick, and process the wool into yarn or batting in an hour. The same job done at home would take a week. The Wile facility could be said to be an early contribution to the concept of working smarter, not harder.

Women laboured for long hours in this mill, where wool was made into batts and carded for spinning, knitting, and weaving.

(902) 543-8233
Open June 1–Sept. 30
Mon.–Sat. 9:30–5:30
Sun. 1–5:30

Directions: The museum is located at 242 Victoria Road, Bridgewater.

Discover Nova Scotia Museums and Art Galleries

Fisheries Museum of the Atlantic & Lunenburg Art Gallery

When European explorers first came to the new world, they found the ocean teeming with fish.

Since the Catholic Church sanctioned meatless Fridays and most of Europe was then Catholic, there was a huge demand for fish from Newfoundland and Nova Scotia.

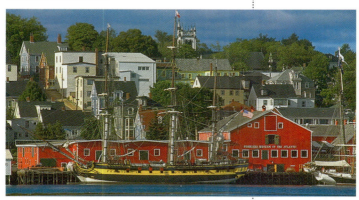

The Fisheries Museum of the Atlantic, housed in a series of bright red buildings along Lunenburg's harbour, is the largest collection in the region devoted to this industry. There is an aquarium, an extensive collection of small wooden boats, and displays of the various gear used by fishermen. Special features are the *Bluenose* collection, the fishing vessels tied to the wharf, and the rum runners display which chronicles the saga of how rum was "smuggled" into international waters along the American coast.

The Fisheries Museum of the Atlantic smells and sounds like the sea. It's a real bluenose experience.

Just a block from the museum is the Lunenburg Art Gallery where shows change every month and an exhibition of local artists is featured each season. The gallery has a small permanent collection by Earle Bailey, a well-known quadriplegic artist who used brush-in-mouth to paint.

Directions: Located on the Lunenburg waterfront, the museum is difficult to miss. The art gallery is at 19 Pelham Street.

The Fisheries Museum lines the picturesque Lunenburg waterfront.

Museum
(902) 634-4794
Open mid-May–Oct. 15
daily 9:30–5:30
Gallery is open April–Oct. 31
Summer hours daily 10–5:30,
other months closed Sun. & Mon.,
open 10–4:30

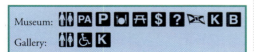

Ross Farm Museum

Billed as Nova Scotia's "Living Museum of Agriculture," Ross Farm chronicles the province's agricultural and rural histories. This is a working history farm. Crops are harvested, products like barrels, lathes, and shingles are produced on site, and heritage farm animals graze in the pastures. To complete the picture, staff dress in a sort of 1870s Mennonite style (the period the farm represents).

Children can take part in the work of nineteenth-century farm life.

Ross Farm not only rekindles memories, it tracks the history of the community of New Ross (it was settled by de-mobbed soldiers in 1817), and the province's early agricultural-based economy. Among the buildings to explore are the Ross family homestead Rose Bank Cottage, Cooper Shop, stave mill, and blacksmith shop. The farm museum shows that agriculture is more than planting seeds and waiting for harvest. It is about hard work, ingenuity, invention, and understanding the natural environment and climate.

Wagon rides at Ross Farm evoke nostalgia.

In the transportation barn visitors see the precursor to the department store—the peddler's wagon, a cramped travelling store which went across the country—and how regional wagons, like the Valley, Colchester and Lunenburg, developed to meet the specific needs of each area. Another barn contains a far-reaching display of quixotic labour-saving instruments like potato sprouters, turnip pulpers or the McCormick Reaper, which looks like a windmill that fell over and went berserk. A collection of ploughs shows how they were adapted to handle different soil conditions.

(902) 689-2210
Open year-round
June 1–Oct.15
daily 9:30–5:30
Jan. 2–March 15
weekend events.
Call for other times.

In a way, Ross Farm is both familiar and exotic because, while it shows us what we think we know and remember, it encourages us to re-examine what we've forgotten.

Directions: The Ross Farm is located on Highway 12, in New Ross (between Chester Basin and Kentville).

William E. deGarthe Gallery

Peggy's Cove attracts tourists and artists for the same reasons: natural light, landscape, and rugged beauty of the sea, whether it's at rest or tempestuous. William deGarthe was one of the artists drawn here, like a moth to light.

In 1994 an addition was built to his seaside cottage to house the William E. deGarthe Gallery. It's a charming, warm, truly Nova Scotian collection. Inside are sixty-five of his paintings and sculptures—worked in oils, acrylics, watercolour, clay, plaster, marble, and cast bronze. Outside, the deGarthe yard is dominated by a massive boulder that deGarthe chiselled into the 30.5 m (100 ft.) long *Fishermen's Memorial*. In three vignettes titled Work, Bounty and Grace, the memorial portrays the fishing life.

William deGarthe was captivated by the story of a shipwrecked orphan girl, "Peggy of the Cove," for whom the Cove was named. He painted her in styles as varied as Botticeilli's *Birth of Venus* to the Dali-like *Pax in Terra*.

On the surface, deGarthe's work is conventional. And it may even be underrated because of his output—he completed as many as 350 canvases in one year! Yet, it inspires debate. Some works have a strong spiritual aspect even though deGarthe claimed not to be religious.

Technique aside, a deGarthe constant is respect for hard work. His most poignant painting is *The Phoebe*. His wife, Phoebe, was so upset when he sold this work he repainted the scene, put her name on the ship's bow, and, in a final act of contrition, hid an embracing couple in the clouds. It was one of the last paintings he completed before his death.

Surprises, secrets, and contradictions make the deGarthe Collection worth the drive.

Directions: Head to Peggy's Cove on Trans-Canada Highway 103, then follow the Lighthouse Route to the village.

Peggy's Cove is one of Nova Scotia's many scenic coastal villages that exude Maritime charm.

William E. deGarthe carved his *Fishermen's Memorial* from a granite outcropping behind his house.

(902) 823-2256
Open mid-May, Sept.& mid-Oct. 9:30–5:30;
June–Aug. 9:30–6

Index

Acadia University Art Gallery 14
Admiral Digby Museum 5
Age of Sail Heritage Centre 26
Alexander Graham Bell National Historic Site 38–39
Anna Leonowens Gallery 66
Anne Murray Centre 24
Argyle Township Courthouse and Gaol 85
Art Gallery of Nova Scotia 65
Atlantic Canada Aviation Museum 69
Balmoral Grist Mill 32
Barrington Woolen Mill, 87
Black Cultural Centre for Nova Scotia 77
Canso Museum 60–61
Cole Harbour Heritage Farm 82
Cossit House 52
Cumberland County Museum 30
Dalhousie Art Gallery 68
DesBrisay Museum 93
Evergreen House 78–79
Firefighters' Museum of Nova Scotia 3
Fisheries Museum of the Atlantic 95
Fisherman's Life Museum 56
Fort Anne National Historic Site 6
Fort Edward National Historic Site 16
Fortress Louisbourg National Historic Site 46–48
Fundy Geological Museum 25
Gallerie Père-Leger-Comeau 4
Glace Bay Miners' Museum 50
Grand Pré National Historic Site 15
Grassy Island National Historic Site 60–61
Great Hall of the Clans 42
Haliburton House 19
Halifax Citadel National Historic Site 70–71
Hank Snow Country Music Centre 92
Hector Exhibit and Research Centre 33
Hector Heritage Quay 33
Heritage Model Centre 22
HMCS *Sackville* 72
J. C. Williams Dory Shop 88–89
Jost House Museum 52
Lawrence House 28
Les Trois Pignons/Elizabeth Le Fort Gallery 41
Lunenburg Art Gallery 95
Lyceum, the 52
Macdonald Museum 10
Marconi National Historic Site 51
Margaree Salmon Museum 40
Maritime Command Museum 64
Maritime Museum of the Atlantic 73
McCulloch House 33
Mount Saint Vincent University Gallery 67
North Hills Museum 8
Nova Scotia Highland Village 43–44
Nova Scotia Museum of Industry 35–36
Nova Scotia Museum of Natural History 74–75
O'Dell House 7
Old Burying Ground, the 76
Old Kings Courthouse Museum 11
Old Meeting House, the (Barrington) 86
Orangedale Railway Station Museum 45
Perkins House 90
Port Royal National Historic Site 9
Prescott House 12
Quaker House 78–79
Queens County Museum 90
Randall House 13
Regional Museum of Cultural History 78–79
Ross Farm Museum 96
Ross-Thomson House and Store 88–89
Shand House 17
Shearwater Aviation Museum 80–81
Shelburne County Museum 88–89
Sherman Hines Museum 91
Showcase Nova Scotia 27
Sherbrooke Village 57–59
Sobey Collection of Canadian Art 34
Springhill Miners' Museum 23
St. Mary's Church 4
St. Patrick's Church 52
St. Paul's Cemetery 76
Sutherland Steam Mill Museum 31
Sydney and Louisbourg Railway Museum 49
Wedgeport Sport Tuna Fishing Museum 84
Wile Carding Mill Museum 94
William E. deGarthe Gallery 97
Windsor Hockey Heritage Museum 18
Uniacke Estate Museum Park 20
University College of Cape Breton Art Gallery 54
Yarmouth County Museum Complex 2